PRAISE FOR

CRYSTAL MUSE

"*Crystal Muse* is pure enchantment. It is written with grace, deep knowledge, and the kind of magic that comes only from years and years of experience trusting and working in the unseen realms. I highly recommend this book to everyone who wants to live a more delightful and fulfilling life."

— **CHRISTIANE NORTHRUP, M.D.**
New York Times best-selling author of *Goddesses Never Age*

"My connection with crystals began on a journey to a red rock on a spiritual vortex in Sedona, AZ. I now have a crystal altar in my home and place them around my yoga mat during practice. Each crystal is a gift of patience and self-love. In a chaotic time, *Crystal Muse* shares how connecting to the calm, grounding energy of crystals can help us engage with each other and ourselves."

— **LENA DUNHAM**
actress, writer, and filmmaker

"Heather and Timmi offer up simple, powerful rituals that make it easy to tune in to the energy of the Universe on a daily basis. Their breakdowns demystify crystals and help you incorporate them into your everyday life for miraculous results."

— **GABRIELLE BERNSTEIN**
#1 *New York Times* best-selling author of
The Universe Has Your Back

"I'm a believer that a healthy lifestyle begins with a healthy mind. *Crystal Muse* has taught me how to use crystal energy to shift my mindset . . . so I'm prepared for whatever my day throws at me (even with the chaos that comes with being a super-momma of three!)."

— **MOLLY SIMS**
mom, actress, and author

"A must-read for any crystal curious soul to a fully-fledged gemstone junkie. Pages full of practical rituals, easy-to-read crystal meanings, and how-tos make this book my new crystal go-to."

— **EMMA MILDON**
international best-selling author of
The Soul Searcher's Handbook

"Finally! A crystal book that explains how to use your crystals in the now age. With simple, crystallized rituals that can be done in under 11 minutes, *Crystal Muse* will take you on a journey within to transform your life from the inside out."

— **JASON WACHOB**
founder and CEO of mindbodygreen and author of *Wellth*

"This colorful book will become your crystal bible! A must for enthusiasts and the crystal curious alike."

— **RUBY WARRINGTON**
founder of The Numinous and author of
Material Girl, Mystical World

"Packed with energy, insight, and patience, crystals are a result of the Earth's eternal transformation and therefore can offer deep wisdom and profound healing, and be brilliant reminders of our own transformation. *Crystal Muse* bridges the gap between books about wellness and books about crystals with a blend of practical, crystal energy techniques for personal betterment."

— **JASON MRAZ**
singer and songwriter

"So many of my blog readers (and myself!) have shown a huge interest in crystals—what they do for us, how to enjoy them, how to soak in their magic, and so much more. Finally, two amazing humans break it down for us in an approachable, reader-friendly, and realistic way! Heather and Timmi have created a space where we can all enjoy the ancient mysticism of crystals in the current age."

— **JORDAN YOUNGER**
founder of The Balanced Blonde and author of
Breaking Vegan

"*Crystal Muse* offers health, support, and healing assistance for humans old and young looking to increase inner and outer glow and growth."

— **JILL WILLARD**
intuitive and author of *Intuitive Being*

"Fashion is all about creating a moment. The crystal rituals in *Crystal Muse* help me to be present today so that I can design the fashions of tomorrow."

— **MARY ALICE HANEY**
fashion designer, creative director, and CEO of Haney

"Working in the music industry and being a mother of three can be, at times, stressful. The crystal rituals of *Crystal Muse* give me peace of mind no matter how crazy my day gets."

— **JODY GERSON**
chairman and CEO of Universal Music Publishing Group

CRYSTAL MUSE

CRYSTAL MUSE

EVERYDAY RITUALS
TO TUNE IN TO THE REAL YOU

HEATHER ASKINOSIE and **TIMMI JANDRO**

HAY HOUSE, INC.

Carlsbad, California • New York City
London • Sydney • New Delhi

For all the crystal lovers, soul seekers, trailblazers,
visionaries, light workers, and spiritually curious.
This one's for you.

This book was blessed by:
Lama Tsering Wangdu Rinpoche
Amma Sri Karunamayi

CONTENTS

INTRODUCTION

HOW TO USE THIS BOOK

Crystal Muse: Everyday Rituals to Tune In to the Real You has been designed just for you. Within these pages, we are going to show you practical ways to tap into your highest potential. How? With crystals, of course!

Each chapter offers a series of simple rituals that you can use to help transform your life. These rituals reflect years of study and hands-on experience with some of Earth's most magical gifts. These are the formulas that have worked best for us. Once you become familiar with the stones, you may want to come up with some rituals of your own. Always trust your intuition and inner guidance. Remember, you know yourself better than anyone.

Think of this as a crystal recipe book—one that you can skim through or read cover to cover. Scan through the chapter titles, and if one of them catches your eye, take note. It may be your higher self calling out to you to investigate the ritual, or perhaps your curiosity is prompting you to read more.

Timmi and I are thrilled to share some of our adventures with you. From the beginning of our business, Energy Muse, we have had different roles. I've been in charge of the crystal expertise and creative side of things, while Timmi has been in charge of production and operations. While my voice will be your guide throughout this book, it is our journeys together that have been the privilege of a lifetime. We hope they will encourage you to delve more deeply into your life so that you may discover ways to live up to your own highest potential.

Now, let's start talking crystals!

— HEATHER ASKINOSIE

CHAPTER 1

MY AHA MOMENT WITH CRYSTALS

"Being crystal clear is the new super power."
— HEATHER ASKINOSIE,
crystal expert and holistic healer

I HAVE BEEN WORKING WITH CRYSTALS FOR OVER 25 YEARS. IN THAT TIME, I HAVE SEEN LIVES TRANSFORMED. I HAVE WATCHED FINANCES AND health improve. I've witnessed new romances, the healing of old wounds, and the release of negative belief systems. I've even observed women conceiving after years of struggle.

Crystals are an Earth tool. Like a beautiful garden or a glorious beach, crystals can inspire you to slow down and remember your essence. In this busy world, we can sometimes forget all the wonderful things that already exist within us. Working with crystals will help you remember.

Before I began my journey with crystals, I thought I had everything. By conventional standards, I did. I grew up in a small beach town in Southern California. It was an environment filled with free spirits. My parents surrounded themselves with a diverse group of friends, and from a young age I was exposed to an expansive way of thinking. My grandmother would read my tea leaves, and every year I'd get an astrology reading. My mother would clear our house with sage and follow the different stages of the Moon. But even within this open-minded community, I was still never introduced to crystals.

After college, I got my real estate license, and for a long time, life was easy. I had my family, good friends, a house by the beach, money, no commitments—everything I needed. Until one day, I stumbled upon an obscure store that had just opened down the street. Peering into the window, I was confused by the strange objects that I saw. I hesitated to go inside, but curiosity (something I have an abundance of) got the best of me. From the moment I walked through the door, I felt as if I had entered another world—one filled with enchantment, color, wisdom, and most especially, *secrets*.

The shelves were stocked with soaps, oils, and rocks—lots and lots of rocks. I pointed to one and said, "This is the most beautiful thing I have ever seen."

The store owner had heard me. "It's an Amethyst crystal from Brazil, and it emits a calming energy," she said. "Pick it up, and hold it in your hands. Feel its vibration."

I had absolutely no idea what she was talking about. Crystals? Energy? Vibration? What did she mean? She must have seen the confused look on my face because before I knew what was happening, she walked over, placed the crystal in my hands, and wrapped my fingers around its cool surface.

"Just feel it," she said.

So I did. I held it in my hands and felt it. Then I picked up another one, and then another, and stayed until the store closed.

From that day on, I began to live a double life. I was a successful real estate agent by day, but all my free time was spent in that little store with the rocks. Something profound was happening within me. It was as if the energy of the crystals was pulling me into their world. I was enchanted by them. At times, I wished I could push pause on my "real life" so that I could spend more time with these incredible rocks.

I had to know more about each one, just as I would a new friend. "Where are you from?" I'd ask. "Brazil? Peru? Madagascar?" The store owner told me that every one of them was unique and emitted a vibrational energy that could act as a tool to awaken, shift, and transform one's life. But how could a rock do this? And if it were true, why weren't more people talking about this ancient secret? Although the skeptic in me doubted, the curious researcher in me eventually won out. I purchased a few crystals and placed them around my house.

At first, I just stared at them. But then I began holding my Amethyst before I went to sleep each night. It was as if a little world of energy that I couldn't see with my naked eye was living inside of it. I became a human sponge, seeking out any information I could find on crystals. I purchased one of the few books that were available at the time and read it cover to cover in a single sitting. The next day, I called the author and asked if she'd be willing to talk to me more about crystals. Within the week, I boarded a plane to the Big Island of Hawaii. My journey with crystals had officially begun.

Soon, working with crystals became all consuming. The money I made selling real estate was invested in traveling across the globe to meet shamans, healers, energy workers, and Feng Shui masters. When my friends asked me to join them on a night out, my standard excuse became, "Sorry, I can't. I've already made plans with my crystals." Yes, my friends thought I was off my rocker. But I knew the crystals were leading me on a magical journey, and that I was finally feeling fully alive.

Although my journey with crystals has been liberating, empowering, and humbling, it has also been challenging. I started dabbling in the crystal world way before it became mainstream—now you can buy a crystal at Target! I was called everything from a "witch" to a "weirdo." (Twenty-five years later, people still call me these things, but now that I am older and wiser, I think of them as compliments.)

Being on any spiritual path is not for the

faint of heart. Some days it's easier to just avoid the internal struggle that comes with it. And sometimes, it can be lonely. In those early days, I often found myself traveling to remote places to meet with healers and medicine men in the jungles of Belize, or trekking to retreat centers in the middle of Bali. But even in those most lonesome of days, I felt comforted by the Earth's energy and by the vibrant plants and ancient rocks that surrounded me.

Much of the information that was shared with me about crystals and their healing properties was given verbally. I had experienced crystals grids on my body and medicine wheels of stones in the middle of the desert. But now it was time to take all that I had learned and share it. Long before it became popular, I began massaging people with crystals and hot rocks. I secretly placed crystals in the homes I sold to balance the energy of the property. I gave crystals to my friends and asked them to report back to me any changes or breakthroughs they may have had. The greatest joy for me soon became watching others prosper from the secrets I was sharing with them.

This meant I had a decision to make: Should I walk forward into the unknown and fully commit to learning the secret rituals of crystal healing? Or should I stay huddled and safe in the crazy but successful world of real estate? I still had bills to pay, after all, and the money I had saved would soon run out.

I chose the crystals—or perhaps they chose me. I took the path of a loner, an adventurer, and a seeker of truth. I spent hours upon hours with crystals, which I had begun to think of as "wisdom keepers." My life had changed forever.

It was cool. It was liberating. It was hard.

As my friends bought homes and started families, I bought crystals. People didn't understand me, and at times I didn't understand myself. How had I turned out like this? My parents didn't raise me, send me to college, and give me a solid foundation so that I would end up being a crystal energy healer. A wise woman once told me, "It's not an easy journey that you are on, but it will end up being the most rewarding." She was right.

Perhaps my biggest reward came in the form of my childhood best friend, Timmi. While I was off on my crystal journeys, Timmi was working her way up in the garment industry. She was a salesperson extraordinaire, and I could not have been more proud of my best friend's success. When she suggested we collaborate, I was overjoyed. We made a natural team. She had the production know-how, and I had the crystal secrets. And our crystal energy–based company, Energy Muse, was born.

Our business has evolved from offering intentional crystal jewelry to creating global awareness about the benefits of crystals, demystifying their "woo-woo" reputation and how to use them in simple daily rituals. We have spent decades developing relationships with crystal miners from all over the world to find crystals that are ethically sourced and hold the highest vibrations. Every day, we are working to help people remember their own personal power by tapping into the purest energy of all—Mother Earth.

"Love is in the Earth."

— MELODY,
crystologist

CHAPTER 2

CRYSTAL CRASH COURSE

EVERYTHING YOU NEED TO KNOW ABOUT USING CRYSTALS

"I find when I give myself gifts—the gift of time, the gift of self-forgiveness, the gift of letting go—I thrive. For me, crystals are a representation of all that—an object whose beauty and energy both remind me to step back, thank the world, thank my body. The weight of a crystal in my hand or around my neck resets me, connects me to something ancient and reminds me that I am worthy of beautiful moments and beautiful things, each unique and sparkling."

— LENA DUNHAM,
writer and filmmaker

TAKE A LOOK AT ALL THE CRYSTALS ON PAGE 9, AND TAKE NOTE OF WHICH ONES YOU LINGER ON. CIRCLE THE FIRST THREE STONES that you are attracted to. Please don't overthink it; just pick your favorite three stones in this moment.

Once you've picked your three stones, you can read the meaning of each one on the following page.

There. See how easy that was? You've just officially started working with crystals.

Very often, the crystals you choose will be absolutely relevant to your life in the present moment. It's your intuition's way of telling you what your soul needs. Isn't it crazy how accurate the crystals are? Truthfully, it's how accurate *you* are. Remember that *you* picked the stones! Something deep within your soul was telling you what you needed to remember about yourself.

WHAT CAN CRYSTALS DO FOR YOU, REALLY?

All of us feel the need to connect. But connect to what, exactly? The Mayans looked to the stars to connect to time, the seasons, and the cycles of life. Many Indian chiefs tell stories of the wind, the four directions, two-legged beings, four-legged animals, plant and rock people, swimmers, crawlers, and the Great Spirit to show our universe is interconnected. The indigenous shamans taught of the healing properties of plants and how they can be used to remedy many of our ailments on Earth. The saints and sages shared their views of wisdom and hope, and how faith can create bonds between us.

In the *now* age, a four-inch screen connects us to information and each other within seconds, but at the same time, it disconnects us from Mother Nature's wisdom. Mother Nature is real. She's all around us and she is our true connector.

So, how do we push the reset button and reconnect? There's a part within your soul that says, "Stop, breathe, and listen; you have everything you need within yourself." It reminds you that you can find peace even in the midst of chaos. Crystals can help you do that.

Mystics and ancient wisdom keepers often referred to crystals as "the stone people." They believed that within each crystal, there is a story and a spiritual message. Many crystals have been nestled deep within the Earth for millions of years. As a result, they hold the imprint of life and the Earth's evolution within their walls. They act as mini record keepers. This is why they are known as the Earth's messengers and wisdom keepers.

Crystals teach us to connect through silence. Each stone has its own unique blueprint. The process of tapping into a crystal's vibration is similar to how we tap into our own—with stillness.

Crystals are neutral. They have no judgments, opinions, or worries. They may contain ancient knowledge, but they are 100 percent present in the now. They don't interpret a situation as good or bad. (That's what we as humans do.) A crystal doesn't care what religion you believe in, and it doesn't care about your sexual preference or political viewpoints either. It doesn't care how much money you make, how spiritually evolved you are, what your IQ is, or about your ethnicity. Imagine how amazing it would be if we could adopt this same ability to withhold judgment!

Crystals don't ask to be worshipped or prayed to, but they do have information waiting to be accessed.

Crystals have been part of the Earth since the beginning of time, so even if they're new to *your* world, *you're* not new to theirs. If I could take my 25-plus years of connecting with crystals and interpret their message, it would be this: As a society, humans are continuously looking forward. It's always about bigger, better, faster, and more. Maybe it's time to slow down and notice that many of the answers we seek are just below our feet, nestled into the Earth that we share.

Relationships are everything to us. We depend on them to survive. But it's not only our relationships to each other that buoy us; it's also our relationship to our planet. For some of us, it might be time to reestablish this connection. Holding a crystal in your hand or placing them in your environment can help you remember that you are part of something bigger—something that's been around for millions of years.

Carnelian Creativity Confidence Motivation	**Rhodochrosite** Self-Worth Love Joy	**Rhodonite** Love Power Generosity	**Rose Quartz** Love Beauty Happiness	**Garnet** Health Passion Energy flow	**Red Jasper** Stability Grounding Healing
Picture Jasper Nurturing Stability Earth	**Agate** Strength Healing Inner power	**Rutilated Quartz** Guidance Angels Healing	**Pyrite** Abundance Luck Reflects negativity	**Citrine** Happiness Light Success	**Mookaite** Adventure Willpower True potential
Tree Agate Abundance Centering Peace	**Jade** Wealth Wisdom Prosperity	**Malachite** Love Transformation Balance	**Aventurine** Luck Optimism Wealth	**Green Calcite** Prosperity Balance Clearing	**Chrysoprase** Love Compassion Kindness
Aquamarine Tranquility Peace Release	**Bloodstone** Courage Self-esteem Energy	**Chrysocolla** New Beginnings Power Soothing	**Kambaba Jasper** Inspiration Overcoming fears	**Ocean Jasper** Happiness Uplifting Joy	**Rhyolite** Creativity Change Positivity
Celestite Uplifting Calming Releases stress	**Blue Lace Agate** Calming Peace of mind Relaxation	**Sodalite** Harmony Communication Healing	**Dumortierite** Patience Guidance Insight	**Lapis Lazuli** Enlightenment Awareness Wisdom	**Apatite** Creativity Inspiration Ambition
Tiger's Eye Wealth Optimism Success	**Smoky Quartz** Grounding Transmutation Releases fear	**Leopard Skin Jasper** Self-Healing Grounding Stability	**Amethyst** Spirituality Intuition Peace	**Botswana Agate** Peace Serenity Healing	**Fluorite** Clarity Cleansing Rejuvenation
Black Tourmaline Cleansing Protection Absorbs negativity	**Shungite** Detoxifying Purifying Protection	**Onyx** Protection Blocks negativity	**Labradorite** Higher Consciousness Intuition	**Hematite** Grounding Balance Earthing	**Bronzite** Protection Stabilizing Self-esteem
Clear Quartz Clarity Manifestation Focus	**Selenite** Cleansing Healing Protection	**Moonstone** Harmonizing Protection Fertility	**Dalmatian Jasper** Happiness Playfulness Positivity	**Tourmalinated Quartz** Luck Wealth Balance	**Abalone** Calming Soothing Healing

WHY CRYSTALS WORK

"Do crystals really work?" I am asked that a lot. My answer is always the same: "They do for me!"

First of all, they make me happy when I look at them. I place them all around my house to remind me to always be grateful for Mother Nature's beauty. As soon as I hold a crystal in my hand, I feel grounded. I remember to breathe. It isn't a placebo effect. It isn't in my head. It's a tangible shift in my energy—an overwhelmingly good one.

Second, almost every ancient civilization since the beginning of time has used crystals in a variety of ways—from healings to offerings to protective talismans. Queen Cleopatra and the ancient Egyptians used ground Malachite and Lapis Lazuli to create a rainbow of eye shadows and cosmetics. The Romans embedded crystals into their armor and shields to provide protection and strength while in battle. In India, Ayurvedic medicine has used crystal energy to correct physical, emotional, and metaphysical imbalances within the body. So while we might not know *exactly* how a crystal works, we know we're not the only ones who believe in them. The truth is we wouldn't still be in business if they didn't work.

Crystals have an orderly structure, known as a *crystal lattice*. The energy they emit remains at a constant frequency. When a crystal is placed on or near an area of the body emitting at a lower frequency, it encourages the body to match its higher frequency. So on the most basic level, when you're feeling low, bringing a crystal into your energy field helps to lift you up.

If you're still not convinced, think of it this way: Quartz has made the digital world a reality. Consider all the devices you use in a day—your cell phone, tablet, and computer. Did you know that LCD stands for liquid crystal display and that every one of these devices is powered by a silicon processor chip? Silicon is an element derived from silicate minerals, a.k.a. Quartz, found in the Earth's crust.

The silicon chip in your computer has been programmed to store several hundred gigabytes of information. Thus, isn't it conceivable that a crystal could transform other energies as well? That our intentions and thoughts might even be influenced by a crystal's subtle vibration?

Using the healing power of crystals as a tool for empowerment, balance, and enlightenment is directly related to your own personal belief. If you believe that crystals will help you on an energetic and vibrational level, they most certainly will. If instead you're thinking, *They won't work since science hasn't proven they will*, you're still correct—they probably won't work for you. For crystals to work, you have to approach them with an open mind and a willingness to work with them to accomplish your goals. Look at it this way: while science still has yet to prove that crystals can affect our mental and physical being, neither has it proven that they can't.

HOW DO I CHOOSE A CRYSTAL?

Whether you're headed to your local metaphysical store or browsing online, the first step to choosing your crystal is to get out of your head and into your heart. It's important to trust yourself. We're confident you'll know which crystal is right for you. How? Because you know

yourself better than anyone else. As you pick up a variety of crystals, some will feel light, while others will feel heavy. You'll be drawn to some, and you'll pass over others. It might be the color, the shape, or the size that makes you pause on one and not the other. None of these specifics matter. This is your intuition talking to you.

Once you've narrowed it down to a handful of crystals, how do you decide which one?

Take a closer look. Notice the layers and inclusions, the flaws and imperfections inside each crystal. Which one fascinates you the most? Which one is the most beautiful to you? Which one draws you in deeper, asking you to take a closer look? This is the crystal that is right for you.

It's also important to note that different crystals ignite different feelings for different people. For example, one crystal may emit the energy of tranquility for one person, and that same crystal might be energizing for someone else. This is why in the rituals to follow, it's important to focus on aligning your intention with your crystals and developing your own relationship with each stone rather than being told what the crystal is supposed to bring you. It's less about the properties each crystal has been known to carry and more about how you, as an individual, respond to it. Similarly, the same crystal can magnify different energies in different situations. In one ritual, a crystal might be used to help in moving forward on a new path, while in another it may be used to help in releasing the past.

I GOT MY CRYSTAL. NOW WHAT DO I DO?

There are several paths that you can take to connect with your crystal. As with any worthwhile relationship, you need to invest the time to get to know one another. Your crystal is striving to get to know you, just as you are striving to get to know it.

Take the time to hold it, touch it, and tune in to its frequency. Look at its color, shape, and size. Be aware of any sensations that come up while you are holding it. You may experience a tingling or warmth in your hands. Take note of any specific emotions that may arise as well. Is it happiness, sadness, or joy? There's no wrong or right way to feel in the presence of your crystal, and everyone's experience will be unique.

What if you don't feel anything when you hold your crystal? Then, at this time, you don't feel anything! It's that simple. Try not to judge the experience—just *be* with it. Sometimes it may take a while for a certain crystal to resonate with you, while at other times that same crystal will make the hairs on your arms stand up.

We suggest that no matter what happens, you open your heart to the crystals. See them as a gift from Mother Earth. Open yourself to what comes your way when you work with their energy. Sit with them, breathe, connect, and listen to them. They're waiting patiently for you!

 I've had my crystal for two days. Why isn't it working?

 Does a diet work in two days? Does a fitness regimen work in two days? Like any new program, it takes time and consistency to get results. Working with crystals is no different. The magic is not the crystal; it's *you*. It's not doing the work; you're doing the work. It's an ally on your journey. A tool to help you get to where you want to go.

 What are five simple ways to use my crystal?

- Carry it in your pocket or purse.
- Wear it.
- Place it on your altar or nightstand.
- Lay it on your body.
- Meditate while holding it.

WHAT IS AN INTENTION?

Intentions are like magnets. They attract what will make them come true. Setting an intention is a powerful tool for achieving happiness. Crafting an intention starts by setting goals that align with your values, aspirations, and purpose.

1. Decide what matters to you. Your values drive the actions in your life, and you'll need to recognize what truly matters to you if you want to find fulfillment.

2. Explore areas of your life that need an up-grade. Consider how you can improve your relationships, career, social life, spirituality, health, and community.

3. Be specific about *what* you want to achieve, *when* you want to achieve it, and *why*.

4. Bring your intentions to life. Certain rituals in the following chapters will ask you to write them down. Make sure you write them in the present tense, as if they're happening *now*, and affirm *only* what you want. You should also write down your goal, the end result of what you wish to manifest. Put feeling into it! For example, *"I am a money magnet. Money flows into my life easily and effortlessly."*

HOW DO I PROGRAM MY CRYSTAL?
———

Give your crystal a job and a purpose! One of the most important components to working with crystals is setting an intention, "program-ming" each stone to reflect what it is that you want. It wants to work for you, but you have to tell it what to do. Life doesn't always go as planned, and it can throw you off-kilter. In the moments when you're vibrating at a lower fre-quency, your intentions can fly out the window. When you reconnect with your programmed crystal, it will help you remember your goals and limitless potential.

Programming your crystal is simple. Cleanse your crystal—more to come on that later—hold it in your hands, close your eyes, and take three deep breaths. Reflect on your faith, the Earth, and what makes you happy. This will connect you with your highest vibration. Your highest vibration may be associated with

a religious or spiritual belief, God, or simply a divine power that's greater than you. Or it may be associated with a scientific connection—zero-point energy. You decide what to call it. Then, while in this space of love and light, ask that your crystal be cleared of all unwanted energy and previous programming.

Aloud or in your head, say, *"I ask that the highest vibration of love and light connect with my highest self to clear all unwanted energy and any previous programming. I command this crystal to hold the intention of . . ."* To finish the sentence, add three intentions for your crystal—energies that you wish it to hold for you. End by repeat-ing "thank you" three times. By saying it three times, you emphasize that what you're asking for already exists in the universe.

WHY CRYSTAL RITUALS ARE EFFECTIVE
———

Let's say you want to bake a cake for some-one's birthday. More than likely, you'll follow a recipe that uses specific ingredients and steps to produce the desired result. Just like with food recipes, specific rituals can give you steps to help you create the space you'll need to make room for your intentions.

Think of a crystal ritual as a ceremony in which you can focus on one aspect of your life and elevate it from ordinary to extraordinary. A crystal ritual allows you to combine this focus with the creative power of intention.

Please keep in mind that you don't need to follow any particular faith or religion to take part in any of the rituals in this book.

Q: Can I do multiple crystal rituals at the same time?

A: We recommend working with one crystal ritual at a time before you add in other rituals. We feel it's best to establish a relationship with a crystal or group of crystals first, taking the time to get to know them. Think of it as starting a new relationship with someone; you'll probably want to get to know them a little better before introducing them to your group of friends.

THE IMPORTANCE OF TIMING IN EACH RITUAL

The time it takes for each individual to shift into a ritual state of consciousness varies. We've chosen time frames that have been effective for us. These rituals can last anywhere between 11 minutes and 40 days. We've found that most people are able to focus on something for 3 to 9 minutes without interruption, while 11 minutes pushes the boundaries a little. This is the time when you might begin to feel uncomfortable. It's in this state of slight discomfort that you learn the most about yourself!

CRYSTAL SHAPES AND WHY THEY WORK

Someone new to the crystal world may think the way a stone is cut or shaped is purely aesthetic, but there's a little more to a crystal's shape than meets the eye. While it won't change the type of energy that a crystal gives off, the way a crystal is cut can affect and even enhance how you experience that energy. Think about it in terms of music. You can listen to the same song on a record player, with headphones, or through surround-sound speakers and have a completely different experience with it each time. It's the same song, but the raw texture of a record player, focused feel of headphones, and full-bodied atmosphere of surround sound will all give you different perspectives. Knowing which crystal shape does what will help you amplify your experience based on the mood you're in. Need to focus? Use a crystal point. Looking for some stability? Go for the grounding essence of a cube. You can use specific crystals and shapes for a fit tailored to your energetic needs.

TUMBLED STONES

Tumbled stones are a great place to start your crystal adventure. For a small investment, the benefits you receive from these pocket-sized crystals are significant. We have found that many of our clients will work with a different stone every day, one that they resonate with that acts as their "daily energy prescription." Because of their size, tumbled stones can be put in your pocket or in your bra, displayed on your office desk, placed inside your car, or tucked under your pillow.

SPHERES

Crystal spheres allow energy to emit in all directions. The perfect symmetry of a sphere brings balance, peace, and relaxing energies into its environment. Meditating with a sphere provides a deep sense of wholeness, as if you hold the world in the palm of your hand. They unite all parts of your being and connect you with the energy of your surroundings.

PYRAMIDS

Pyramids are one of the most powerful tools for both manifesting and amplifying energy. This sacred shape has been used by many ancient civilizations, none more famously than the ancient Egyptians. They believed that pyramids symbolized the rays of the Sun. Crystals in this sacred shape are thought to harness high vibrational energies for greater manifestation power.

HARMONIZERS

Crystal harmonizers are polished into cylindrical shapes for holding during meditation. These crystal tools have been crafted for curing energy blocks and energetic imbalances since the time of the ancient Egyptians. By holding one harmonizer in the left hand (yin) and one in the right (yang), spiritual vitality is reinvigorated, and a sense of balance can be restored.

CUBES

Many crystals are found in a cubic formation. The cube shape is associated with the root chakra. Meditating with cubic crystals will help to ground your energy and reconnect you with the powerful energy of the Earth. By placing cubic formations in each of the four corners of a room, you will seal, protect, and ground the energy of your space.

HEARTS

Heart-shaped crystals remind you that you are always surrounded by love. They are powerful allies in helping to attract love from others, as well as nourishing yourself with love from within.

POINTS

Crystal points are one of the most commonly used and beneficial shapes to work with. They are very powerful for manifestation, as they help to manifest your dreams, wishes, and intentions at a much faster rate by directing your intention up into the universe.

CLUSTERS

A crystal cluster occurs when several crystal points grow together on a matrix. Due to the convergence of many crystal points, a crystal cluster vibrates at an even higher energy, directing energy in multiple directions and making it a crystal essential to have in any space.

Traditionally, 40 days is the period of time it takes to break a habit. It's all about consistency! During a 40-day period, you'll learn which days are hardest for you to stay disciplined. Does it get tough on day 15? Day 29? You'll discover your personal breaking point when you start to hold yourself back from succeeding. We encourage you to invest in the specified time suggested for each ritual. This is how you will tap into its highest potential, as well as your own highest potential.

ALIGNING YOUR RITUALS WITH THE PHASES OF THE MOON

You'll notice that many of our crystal rituals begin on the New Moon or the Full Moon. The New Moon marks the beginning of the Moon's cycle and is the ideal time to start new projects and plant new seeds. The Full Moon is when the Moon is at its fullest expression. It's a powerful time to let go of what no longer serves you. (To learn more about living in tune with the Moon, see page 199.)

Now that you have a basic understanding of what the world of crystal energy is all about, you're ready to get started. Hold on tight while we take you on a crystalline adventure! We think it's crystal clear that you're in for an unforgettable journey.

"A time will come when science will make tremendous advances, not because of better instruments for discovering and measuring things, but because a few people will have at their command great spiritual powers, which at the present are seldom used. Within a few centuries the art of spiritual healing will be increasingly developed and universally used."

— GUSTAF STRÖMBERG,
astronomer

CHAPTER 3

SPACE CLEARING

HOW TO CLEAR AND CLEANSE YOUR SPACE, YOUR CRYSTALS, AND YOU

"From a spiritual perspective, letting go of physical 'stuff'
equates with letting go of emotional stuff from your life.
In truth, clutter clearing is never just about the stuff;
it addresses other things going on beneath the surface."

— DENISE LINN,
expert in Feng Shui and space clearing

WHEN YOU FIRST START TO DABBLE IN THE WORLD OF CRYSTALS, YOU WILL QUICKLY REALIZE THAT it's challenging to live in between your new and old world. I tried to hold on to my "old life" for as long as I could, but there came the day that I had no choice. It was time to come out of the crystal closet. I'm hoping that you can make a more graceful entrance into this world than I did!

It happened unexpectedly one morning when I woke up and went through my usual routine. I lit a sage stick and smudged the house in the Native American tradition. This particular morning, however, I used a ceramic pot, filling it to the top with loose sage. Normally, when I fanned my hawk feather over the crackling sage and walked around the house, the smoke would eventually burn out. This time

the loose sage went ablaze. White smoke filled every crevice of empty space in each room. The smoke alarms blared. I ran through the house, opening doors and windows as fast as I could.

My neighbor saw smoke coming from the house and called the fire department. The sirens grew louder and louder. Everyone—and I mean everyone—on my street had come outside to see which house was burning down.

My house filled with so much smoke, I couldn't even see my hand in front of my face. As the firefighters barreled through the front door, they wanted to know, "What's that smell? Where's the smoke coming from?"

"It's a false alarm! I was just saging the house."

My husband, Jason, had already joined my neighbors outside as a spectator, waiting to see what would happen next. (He wanted nothing to do with me at that point!)

The firemen were befuddled. "You're doing *what*?"

"Um. See, the thing is, I'm purifying and cleansing the negative energy in my space and my crystals."

The fireman paused. "With *smoke*?"

"Yup."

"Well then, they're probably pretty purified by now."

My neighbors all had the same looks on their faces—pure shock. But not Jason. He'd probably been wondering when this day would finally come. After the firefighters packed up their hoses and drove away, I tried to explain the situation to the neighbors. It didn't go over well. (My neighbors never did quite understand me.)

That was the day I realized I needed to finally come out of the crystal closet and embrace the spiritual, mystical truth seeker in me.

 How do I know if there's any negative energy in the house, if all seems to be well? Is cleansing even necessary?

 Space clearing is similar to a physical cleaning of your home. Every week, you physically clean your home to keep it neat and tidy. These are other scenarios in which you'd definitely want to clear the energy:

- If there has been a fight or argument
- If someone has been sick
- If things continue to break in the house or you're going through a period of bad luck
- If you've had a big party or a large group of people in your home
- If there's been a recent loss and you've been grieving
- If overall the energy of the space seems heavy and stuck
- When you move into a new home (renting or buying)

YOUR CLEARING AND CLEANSING TOOL KIT

In the crystal rituals within each chapter, you'll notice that the first step includes clearing the energy of your space, your crystals, and you. This process allows you to remove any unwanted and stale energy that may have accumulated over time. Whether you're cleansing your personal energy, the energy of your house, or the energy of your crystals, there are many options available to you. Our go-to tool for cleansing is sage, but there are other methods such as Palo Santo, Frankincense, sea salt, and sound as well.

By using one or a combination of the cleansing tools listed on the upcoming pages, you'll add additional layers of effectiveness to your crystal ritual.

PLEASE NOTE: In the following section, you'll learn the ways that we clear our space. We find these methods to be very effective, but are constantly evolving and shifting how we do so. If you've been trained or have a different belief system in regards to space clearing, always honor that practice.

Sage

Sage is a sacred plant that has been used since ancient times. It's known as a purifier. Burning it before each ritual helps to drive out negative energy and restore balance to a particular space.

How can smudging with sage remove unwanted energy?

"Smudging" with sage is an ancient practice from Native American and other indigenous cultures. It's a purifying "smoke bath" that can be used to cleanse a person, place, object, or space of negative energies or influences. When the smoke begins to melt away, it takes the unwanted energy with it. This can be lower vibrational energy, negative thoughts, or even words from an old argument still hanging in the air. Sage can also be used to purify sacred objects.

Smudging with sage is an easy way to uplift the energy. It's similar to how you might feel when you sit on the sand near the ocean and smell the fresh, salty breeze. That's because moving water and fresh air are natural sources of negative ions, which are actually positive things to have around. The term *negative ion* is an oxymoron because an abundance of it in the air makes you feel better. That's why most of us love the feeling we have after a day at the beach!

The smoke created from burning sage releases a large amount of negative ions into the space. The ending result is a light, balanced, and high vibrational energy. This is why sage is often referred to as "medicine." We highly recommend using sage on yourself and your environment, and always on your crystals before any ritual.

Note that we often use the term *sage* as a verb—you can sage yourself, your space, and your crystals. Some people say "smudge," but either way, it means that you allow the smoke to envelop whatever area you intend to cleanse.

HOW TO USE SAGE

Usually, the sage that's burned is wrapped into a stick, but you can burn individual dried leaves, too. Make sure you have a fireproof container, such as an abalone shell, to catch the ashes. You'll also need a feather to waft the smoke during the cleansing process. Don't let my fire department story scare you! If you follow these steps, you'll be fine (and hopefully your husband won't laugh at you like mine did):

1. Ask the plant-medicine spirit of the sage to be there with you, and ask that it assist in purifying and cleansing you, your space, and your crystals. Hold the sage above the abalone shell as you light it. Let the sage stick catch fire, and allow it to burn for about 30 seconds. Then blow it out.

2. As the smoke wafts from the stick or leaves, first sage yourself using the feather to direct the smoke toward your body. We suggest starting at the top of your head and working downward toward your feet.

3. Sage your space. Open your front door and all the windows in the house to allow the unwanted energy to be released. Starting at the front door, sage around the outside of the door and frame. Now walk back inside, and begin saging the space by moving clockwise through it. Using the feather, waft the smoke into the corners of every room and up to the ceiling. Say these words out loud or silently: *"I ask that the plant spirit of the sage please remove and release any negative energy from this space."*

4. Finally, to clear away any unwanted energy from any hands that have touched your crystals before you, immerse them in the sacred smoke of the sage.

5. When you're finished, extinguish the sage stick by snuffing it out inside of the shell or another fireproof container.

Palo Santo
"THE AROMATIC"

HOW TO USE PALO SANTO:

1. Light your Palo Santo stick.

2. Let the stick catch fire, and allow it to burn for about 30 seconds. Then gently blow it out. If needed, you can blow on the embers to keep the smoke going throughout your cleansing process.

3. Say aloud or silently, *"I ask that the plant spirit of Palo Santo please bring blessings into the space."*

4. To bless yourself, the space, or crystals, simply allow the smoke and rich smell of the Palo Santo to fill the room. To fill your space with blessings, start at the front door and walk clockwise through it with your Palo Santo.

5. When finished, place the Palo Santo stick in a fireproof container. The glow at the end of the stick will eventually go out on its own.

Frankincense
"THE TRANSFORMER"

Palo Santo is another of our favorite energy cleansing tools. Palo Santo means "holy wood" in Spanish. This sacred wood comes from the Palo Santo trees of South America. When it's burned, the smoke is believed to provide medicinal and therapeutic healing energy. Its calming and relaxing aroma is incredible, standing among the greatest of the world's fragrant woods. Because of the extraordinary blessings it bestows upon those who have the good fortune to use it, this wood has touched the hearts and minds of countless people.

Also known as liquid gold or *Boswellia serrata*, this resin is extracted from the Boswellia tree that is found in North Africa, India, and southern Arabia. Frankincense assists in removing negative energy from a space, providing protection, and creating an elevated spiritual awareness. It is often used to lift moods, to ease anxiety and stress, and for purification.

Since Frankincense is a resin, it's best used when placed on top of burning charcoal. Each self-lighting charcoal round has an indentation that serves as the perfect spot for holding the Frankincense in place.

HOW TO USE FRANKINCENSE:

1. Use a fireproof container. This process generates a lot of heat, so if what you're using isn't heavy enough, the heat generated from the charcoal could leave a burned spot.

2. Place the charcoal in your container, and light the top and bottom of the bricks. Wait a few minutes for the charcoal to heat up.

3. Add the Frankincense to the top, and allow the smoke to billow.

4. Say aloud or silently, *"I ask that the plant spirit of Frankincense please purify and uplift the energy of the space."*

5. To cleanse yourself or your crystals, simply allow the smoke and rich smell of the Frankincense to permeate anywhere you wish to clear the energy. To clear the energy of your space, start at the front door and walk clockwise through it with your container.

6. Allow the Frankincense and charcoal to finish burning and smoking. After the smoke evaporates, if the charcoal is still hot, feel free to add more Frankincense to it. Note that the charcoal and the container will remain hot for quite some time even after the smoke has stopped, so be careful when handling them.

Q: I'm moving into a new house. What are the cleansing steps to take? When is the best time to cleanse a space when I am moving?

A: The first thing to do in any space before you move in is to place containers of salt and water in all corners of each room. Ideally this would happen 24 to 48 hours before you move in. Open up all the windows, allowing fresh air and sunlight to fill the space.

Standing at the front door, looking inside your space, state aloud: "To the guardians of [your full address]. My name is _____, and I'm going to be the new occupant here. I would like to introduce myself and ask your assistance in purifying the space of the previous occupants and their energy that might be left behind within the walls, floors, and ceilings." (If it's a completely new house, you would clear the energy of the workers and people who've been in there.) Go through the cleansing process on page 22. You'll also want to clean the floors, windows, and so on with the intention of clearing out all the energies of the previous occupants. On your move-in day, before you begin moving your belongings into your new space, gather all the containers of salt and flush the contents down the toilet.

FENG SHUI TIP: When you move into a new space, the first things you should bring inside are healthy green plants to represent a healthy life, and a jar of honey to bring in sweetness. Always make sure you have a brand-new broom for your new house. You *do not* want to bring an old broom into your new space. You want to start fresh and not be sweeping old debris and memories into your new space.

Sea Salt

"SPIRITUAL CLEANSING AGENT"

Since ancient times, salt has been used to pre-serve and flavor foods, but did you know that it also absorbs negative energy? It's the perfect tool to cleanse and purify your environment. It is also a strong energy tool to repel unwanted spirits.

HOW TO USE SEA SALT:

1. Pour one part water to one part sea salt into four small containers.

2. Place the containers in the four corners of any room. Leave them there for at least 24 hours. The combination of water and sea salt will absorb any negativity and unwanted energy.

3. After 24 hours, pour the contents into the toilet and flush away all the absorbed energy.

4. Repeat this as needed to keep the energy of your space clean and clear.

SOUND:
"PURIFYING VIBRATIONS"

A powerful way to clear and purify space is through sound. You can use your hands by clapping, ringing bells, or beating a drum. By making noise, you wake up any stale energy that may be lingering in the corners. Which-ever sound you decide to use, make sure you do it three times in each corner. Start at your front door and then move around each room in your house in a clockwise direction. This will wake up any stagnant energy and get it flowing again. For a quick and easy energy cleanse, play an *om* mantra or Beethoven's Fifth Symphony in the rooms that need to be "freshened up" a bit.

 Q: I've moved into my partner's house, where he used to live with his ex. I am constantly ill and have no energy. Neither of us is happy here, and I constantly feel depressed and down the minute I walk in the door. When I am outside the house, I feel great, but my mood changes the second I return. What should I do?

 A: Both of you need to go through your house together. Anything that your partner bought with his ex ideally would be removed. It's important to go through the entire house and have an open dialogue about how you feel about the space. Maybe it's time to make some changes, such as a new paint color on the walls, artwork, or a few new pieces of furniture. After you and your partner have decided what changes you want to make, do the Space Clearing Ritual on page 31.

FENG SHUI TIP: If you've gone through a divorce or a very serious breakup, the partner who keeps the mattress is said to be the one who takes longer to get over the relationship— because they're sleeping on the memories of the past. Ideally, if you can, you want to get rid of the mattress and sheets.

A secret for anyone who's had different people sleeping in their bed, a major breakup, or a divorce, and doesn't want to get rid of the mattress: Strip your bed of everything—all the sheets, down to the bare mattress. Open all the windows to get as much light in the room as possible. Fill four glass jars with one part water to one part salt, and place on the floor at the four corners of your bed. Gather the petals of two to three dozen white roses and spread them over the top of the mattress. Keep them there all day. They will purify the energy of past relationships. Next, sage and purify the space. Collect all the petals and give them back to the Earth. Pour all the con-tents from the jars into the toilet and flush.

Selenite

COLOR: White to colorless, transparent to translucent

ORIGIN: Mexico, Morocco, and the U.S.

HISTORY AND LORE: Scientific exploration of the Naica Mine in Chihuahua, Mexico, revealed one of the most magnificent hidden treasures on Earth—a magical cavern filled with white crystals the size of telephone poles and redwood trees. In this mine, 300 meters below the surface, researchers studied Selenite, a variety of gypsum, to shed further light on the origins of life on Earth. Before 2004, gypsum was thought to only exist on our planet. Then it was confirmed that gypsum dune fields existed on the surface of Mars as well. This was exciting news for Mars researchers because the existence of gypsum alludes to the presence of water. This information has also led scientists to believe that there could be the possibility of life on Mars. Maybe that's why its energy feels so out of this world!

HEALING PROPERTIES: The pure, high vibrational energy of Selenite is like liquid light. It has the ability to cleanse, purify, and align you with your highest potential. It shifts your aura and energetic vibration to attune you with a higher energy. Low vibrational energies attract negativity on the same level. Raising your vibration is essential to keeping feelings of grief, fear, anger, and anxiety out of your mental and physical space. Selenite also evokes protection from the angelic realm, helping to dispel all negative energy from the body and mind, as well as bringing deep peace and mental clarity. Selenite crystals will magnify the energy of anything that is placed upon them. Combine them with other crystals to amplify the desired intention.

SPACE CLEARING RITUAL

Your external environment is a mirror image of your internal environment. Clearing the space surrounding you simultaneously clears your mind, body, and spirit. Space clearing is one of the most powerful ways to shift the energy in your life. In less than an hour, your space will feel lighter, happier, and uplifted.

WHAT YOU'LL NEED:

1 sage stick

1 feather

1 abalone shell or fireproof container to catch ashes

1 lighter or matches

1 Palo Santo wood stick to keep the energy grounded and clear while bringing blessings into your space

1 sound maker (bell, drum, chimes) to break up any stagnant or stuck energy

Small glass Mason jars or bowls (enough to place 1 in each room of your space)

Sea salt and Himalayan Salt to absorb any unwanted energy

Black Tourmaline to absorb negative and stagnant energy (enough to place 1 crystal in each room of your space)

Selenite wands to place on the windowsills in each room of the house for cleansing, clearing, protecting, and raising the vibration to a higher level in your environment (enough for at least one windowsill in each room of the house)

1 tray (large enough to hold items above)

OPTIONAL: *Play music during space clearing such as an om mantra, space clearing mantras, or your favorite uplifting music.*

RITUAL STEPS:
Do this space clearing ritual at a time during the day
when you can open the windows.

1. Raise blinds, open your windows, and pull back curtains to allow fresh air and sunshine into the space.
2. Sweep and clean the front doorstep (or entrance into your home) to keep the energy clean, positive, and uplifted.
3. Clean your stovetop. This represents health and your financial life.

4. Hold the Black Tourmaline crystals in your hands, close your eyes, and take 3 deep breaths. Aloud or in your head, say the following: *"I ask that the highest vibration of love and light connect with my highest self to clear all unwanted energy and any previous programming. I command these crystals to hold the intention of absorbing, purifying, and clearing all unwanted energy in this environment. Thank you, thank you, thank you."*

5. Hold the white Selenite wands in your hands, close your eyes, and take 3 deep breaths. Aloud or in your head, say the following: *"I ask that the highest vibration of love and light connect with my highest self to clear all unwanted energy and any previous programming. I command these crystals to hold the intention of light, pure love, and protection. Thank you, thank you, thank you."*

6. Fill the glass Mason jars or bowls with one part water, one part sea salt, and one piece of Black Tourmaline.

7. Place your jars, Selenite crystals, sage, feather, abalone shell, lighter, Palo Santo, and sound maker on the tray.

8. Set your tray down, and grab your sage, feather, abalone shell, and lighter.

9. Starting at the front door, light the sage and say this "Smudge Prayer," given to me by Bobby Lake-Thom (a.k.a. Medicine Grizzly Bear), author of *Native Healer: Initiation into an Ancient Art and Call of the Great Spirit: The Shamanic Life and Teachings of Medicine Grizzly Bear*. You will only say the prayer one time at the beginning of this ritual.

    "Great Creator, the four Powers of the Universe, and all my Relations and Good Spirits in Nature. I come before you in a humble manner and ask for your help. The way I understand it, you put this medicine on the Earth from the Beginning of Creation to help Human Beings. This medicine is used to purify our mind, body, soul, aura, and environment where I now stand. I therefore ask that you accept this medicine and purify me (or anyone else standing close to you as family and friends). I ask that you remove all bad spirits, all bad forces, all ghosts and deceased people, or any evil entities and negative energies. I ask that you remove all fear, pain, and sickness. And do not let them return."

10. Move in a counterclockwise direction around the room, using the feather to guide the smoke to the corners and throughout the room. Place the sage in the abalone shell on the tray after you have finished.

11. Grab the sound maker, and moving in a clockwise direction throughout the room, ring it 3 times in each corner of the room.

12. Place the Mason jar or bowl filled with salt, water, and Black Tourmaline in the center of the room or a place that is safe and where it will be undisturbed.

13. Add your Selenite wands to each windowsill.

14. Take the entire tray into the next room and repeat steps 8 through 13, omitting the prayer.

15. Once all rooms have been cleared, go back to the front door and place the tray on the ground. At this point, all the Selenite should be placed on windowsills, and a jar with your water mixture should be in each room.

16. Light your Palo Santo and state out loud, *"I'd like to bring harmony, happiness, blessings, and good health into my space."* Walk clockwise around your room repeating what energies you'd like to fill the space with. Repeat this in every room of your home. Once you have finished, allow the Palo Santo to burn out on its own.

17. Allow the crystals and the jars to remain in the space for 24 hours.

18. After this time period, go through the rooms and collect all jars.

19. Take the Black Tourmaline out of each jar, rinse it with water, and place it outside in the light of the Sun and Moon for 48 hours to clear and recharge the crystals.

20. Pour all the salt and water down the toilet and flush. Clean the jars and wash your hands.

21. Repeat this ritual as often as needed.

Himalayan Salt

WISDOM KEEPER:
SQUEAKY CLEAN

COLOR: Pale orange

ORIGIN: Pakistan

HISTORY AND LORE: You know salt can combat an icy driveway and even make your well-meaning friend's pot roast bearable, but did you know this miracle mineral could purify your space as well? What *can't* salt do?! Himalayan Salt, or Pink Halite, is similar to the salt in your cabinet—both are composed of mainly sodium chloride. However, the other mineral impurities within it, like magnesium, calcium, potassium, and others, give Himalayan Salt special therapeutic abilities. Himalayan Salt is used as a stress reliever and muscle relaxer in baths, as comforting salt lamps, and in cooking.

HEALING PROPERTIES: Give your space some flavor with Himalayan Salt. It purifies and detoxes energy because of its natural absorbency. Negative energy and a variety of toxins will be soaked up by the salt, leaving behind a cleansed space full of light and positivity.

Q: What can I do quickly on a daily basis to keep my mind, body, spirit, and crystals purified?

A: Light a stick of sandalwood incense with the intention to purify your mind, body, spirit, and crystals of all unwanted energy, and ask that the highest vibration of love and light surround you.

Once you get into a regular routine of clearing and cleansing yourself, your space, and your crystals, it will become second nature. You will become very in tune with yourself and will notice quickly if something feels off or stagnant in your environment. The tools here will assist you in shifting energy quickly and making your rituals more powerful and effective.

"The need for space clearing comes from understanding: we are significantly affected by our surroundings. Uniting Heaven and Earth, we dwell in sacred space."

— Kartar Diamond, Feng Shui master

CHAPTER 4

UNWIND THE MIND

USING MEDITATION TO REFOCUS, RE-CENTER, AND REDUCE ANXIETY

*"Meditation can reintroduce you to that part of
yourself that's been 'missing' for so long."*

— RUSSELL SIMMONS,
spiritual entrepreneur, producer, and author

Y OU'RE AT A FORK IN THE ROAD,"
HE SAID, STARING DIRECTLY
INTO MY EYES.
     I shifted uncomfortably in my
chair. "What do you mean?"

"If you stay on the path you're on, you're
going to crash and burn. It's time to consider
another road if you want to have a fulfilling
life."

Was it that obvious that I had a triple
type-A personality and was spiraling out of
control? So what if my life was busy, and every
minute was accounted for? What's the big deal?

But he was a doctor who specialized in
Ayurveda—the oldest form of preventive health
care on the planet. He was well respected and
had helped other people transform their lives.
I had assumed he'd give me some herbs and a
nutrition program that would help me chill out.

"What do you suggest I do?"

There was a deafening silence for what felt
like an eternity. Until finally he said, "You need
to learn how to meditate."

Scorpios are typically characterized as ex-
tremists. It's all or nothing with us, going from
the highest of highs to the lowest of lows. True
to my nature, I decided to embrace this new
road immediately. Within two weeks, I flew
to a remote area of Canada for a silent retreat
on Transcendental Meditation at Maharishi
International Academy.

Now, bear in mind that this was when I was
in my 20s, before I had explored crystals and
learned much of what I know now. The only
thing I knew about Transcendental Meditation
at that point was that the Beatles had done
it. But I was riddled with anxiety from the
pressures of selling real estate. I wasn't sleeping
enough, and I wasn't nourishing my body with
good foods. And since a friend had also told me

about the retreat, I took that as a sign from the universe that I needed to go.

Upon my arrival, I noticed that everything was very quiet. Silence filled the space—that same deafening silence that I'd experienced in the Ayurvedic doctor's office. I was led to my room, which included a single bed, a teapot, and a view of the lush forest that surrounded us. On the desk lay a sheet of paper with my schedule:

7:30 A.M.	Breakfast
9:00 A.M.	Transcendental Meditation (20 minutes)
10:00 A.M.	Massage
12:30 P.M.	Lunch
3:00 P.M.	Massage
5:30 P.M.	Dinner
7:30 P.M.	Transcendental Meditation Training (20 minutes)

This was my schedule for seven days. If I didn't want to participate in one of the activities, I could choose to take a walk or simply sit in silence. Sounds like heaven, right?

Well, not exactly. For the first three days, it felt like torture. I wanted to talk. I wanted to distract myself from the endless chatter going on in my head. Why did I have to sit at meals with strangers and not talk to them? Was I the only one feeling this way? The only relief I got was when I was allowed to whisper to my Transcendental Meditation teacher.

"How will I know if I'm meditating?" I asked him after my first lesson.

"You'll know," he replied. "Let's begin."

After 30 seconds, I opened my eyes. "Am I there yet?"

"Not yet. Just close your eyes."

I asked the same question every five minutes, only to get the same response: "Not yet. Please, close your eyes." This continued for 20 minutes.

We repeated the same process later that evening. I started to hate it. I dreaded meeting him twice every day. I just wanted to get "there," but I wasn't even close.

For someone who was an overachiever, why was it so damn hard to get "there"? My teacher looked at me with his compassionate eyes and said, "Just give it time." His words bugged me. Even his compassion frustrated me.

By the fifth day, I was over my frustration. Maybe I had surrendered to God. Or maybe it was the fact that I was trapped in this week of silence, in the middle of nowhere, with no way out, and I knew that I had to make the best of it. On that day, I closed my eyes and opened them 20 minutes later. This time, I said nothing. My teacher looked at me and said, "You're there."

I have been a meditator ever since.

WHY MEDITATE?

If you invest in meditation daily, it makes the journey of life easier. It's a powerful tool that can help you handle life, instead of life handling *you*. In the silence of meditation, we can go into the deepest parts of ourselves and connect with something so powerful that it's beyond words. It's a place where we ask questions, knowing the answers will come to us at the perfect time. It's a direct lifeline to the divine and the universe.

Meditation can affect all aspects of your life, allowing you to reflect on how you are living in your world. If your negative thoughts control your mind, those thoughts also control your emotions. We radiate what's inside of us, so those negative thoughts can affect your personality, and might even attract the wrong people to you. As your mind becomes clearer and more peaceful, you will radiate this same energy outward and be better able to attract more positive, uplifting people into your life.

A daily practice of meditation will help you become less reactive. It's empowering to take ownership of the words you say and the choices you make.

We've heard lots of people say, "I can't meditate because I'll do it wrong." But the only wrong way to meditate is to not do it. Of course, the most common excuse is, "I don't have time." There's an old Zen saying: "You should sit in meditation for 20 minutes a day unless you're too busy. Then you should sit for an hour."

Meditation actually gives you more time. It allows you to work smarter instead of harder. Once you stop pushing and *trying* to make things happen, you might find they suddenly just do—without all the stress.

Shungite

WISDOM KEEPER:

THE NEUTRALIZER

COLOR: Black

ORIGIN: Found only in the Karelia area in Russia

HISTORY AND LORE: Touted as the miracle stone of the 21st century, Shungite has been around for an estimated two billion years. It wasn't until the 1996 Nobel Prize–winning research that discovered antioxidant fullerenes within the stone, that people began to wake up to Shungite's healing potential. In Russia, the only location where the stone is found, springs that pass over Shungite rocks were turned into natural spas in the time of Peter the Great. It was believed that Shungite purified the water long before we began using compressed charcoal or carbon blocks in water filters to do the same thing.

HEALING PROPERTIES: Shungite absorbs and eliminates anything hazardous to your body. It is the go-to stone for electromagnetic frequency protection, purification, and detoxification of the body. It also provides a general sense of well-being. Prior to working with Shungite, it's very important that you rinse it under water and place it outside in the Sun for two to four hours. This will clear and recharge its energy.

THE MONKEY MIND RITUAL

TIME FRAME:
11 minutes, as often as needed

The "monkey mind" is a Buddhist metaphor that describes the natural, chaotic state of our untrained minds. The following ritual creates a visual representation of your mind to help you understand the difference between a calm mind and a chaotic one. When you're learning to meditate, this visual helps you understand how easily the mind becomes distracted.

WHAT YOU'LL NEED:

1 small Mason jar filled with water   1 spoonful of dirt

RITUAL STEPS:

1. Observe the clarity of the water in the Mason jar. It's clear and free, with nothing to muddy it.
2. Add a small spoonful of dirt to the water. The dirt represents your thoughts, feelings, fears, and worries. Tighten the lid on the jar and shake it vigorously. This represents how our thoughts and feelings are in a constant state of motion.
3. Look at the water. Is it unclear, distorted, cloudy, and murky? Take a moment to reflect on how this jar is similar to the endless chatter and movement in your mind.
4. Breathe. Watch the dirt slowly settle to the bottom. Breathe. Watch the dirt settle. Breathe. Watch the dirt settle. This is your focused point of attention—watching the dirt settle. Breathe. Watch the dirt settle.
5. Every time your mind becomes hijacked by another thought, idea, or feeling, shake the Mason jar and start over. Go back to your point of attention, watching the dirt settle and breathing. If another thought, idea, or feeling comes into your mind, shake the Mason jar again.
6. Continue this exercise for 11 minutes.
7. Repeat steps 1 through 6 whenever you feel as if you're in a state of chaos.

MEDITATION VORTEX RITUAL

TIME FRAME:
11 to 30 minutes first thing in the morning

When you incorporate crystals into your meditation practice, you take it to the next level. Holding crystals in your hands and surrounding yourself with their energy deepens both your meditation and your connection with the Earth.

Combining the energies of Shungite and Selenite with your daily meditation will create a harmonizing experience that's both grounding and uplifting. As the Shungite works to detox your mind, body, and spirit, the Selenite will soothe and protect you, creating a perfect synergy.

Selenite holds a yin energy of gentleness, softness, transformation, and femininity, while Shungite holds a yang energy of power, logic, control, knowledge, and masculinity. The duality of these energies forms a vortex around you as you meditate, bringing balance to your energy field.

WHAT YOU'LL NEED:

---

4 Shungite cubes to create a vortex of grounding and protective energy around you while you meditate

2 Selenite crystals (a size that fits comfortably in your hands)

to infuse your entire body with light energy

A timer

1 meditation pillow or chair

1 sage stick

1 feather

1 abalone shell or fireproof container to catch ashes from the sage

RITUAL STEPS:

---

1. Sage your environment, and cleanse your crystals (page 22).
2. Sit in a comfortable cross-legged position on the floor with a meditation pillow or in a chair with your feet firmly planted on the floor.
3. Hold the Shungite stones in your hands, close your eyes, and take 3 deep breaths. Aloud or in your head, say the following: *"I ask that the highest vibration of love and light connect with my highest self to clear all unwanted energy and*

any previous programming. I command these crystals to hold the intention of grounding my energy into the Earth. Thank you, thank you, thank you."

4. Put your Shungite crystals to the side, and hold the Selenite crystals in your hands. Close your eyes, and take 3 deep breaths. Aloud or in your head, say the following: *"I ask that the highest vibration of love and light connect with my highest self to clear all unwanted energy and any previous programming. I command these crystals to hold the intention of clearing my energy field and infusing my body, mind, and spirit with liquid light. Thank you, thank you, thank you."*

5. Place 1 piece of Shungite directly in front of you and 1 behind you on the floor. Place another to the right and another to the left of you on the floor. This will create a diamond shape with the Shungite crystals as the points.

6. Place a piece of Selenite in each hand.

7. Set the timer for 11 minutes to 30 minutes—whatever time period feels most comfortable to you.

8. Start to breathe in deeply through the nose and out through the mouth.

9. Breathe out anything you no longer want to hold on to—fear, anger, stress, anxiety, and so on. Visualize the Shungite absorbing all your unwanted energy.

10. Imagine that you're breathing in light. Visualize a ray of white light above your head, showering you with its beam. Visualize a column of white light coming out of the Selenite in each hand to protect each side of your body.

11. Continue until the timer goes off. If other thoughts come into your mind, go back to breathing out unwanted energy and breathing in light.

12. Once a week, cleanse your Shungite of all the unwanted energy it has absorbed during your meditation by running it under water and placing it in direct sunlight for 2 to 4 hours.

13. Cleanse the Selenite every 2 weeks. For more information on how to cleanse your crystals, see page 22.

A MEDITATIVE PRAYER

Chaotic days were becoming the norm for my business partner and best friend, Timmi. On one of these typical days, the phone rang, and the day suddenly became even more chaotic. She heard the panicked voice of her husband: "I think I just blew out my Achilles tendon playing tennis. I need you to take me to the emergency room." She quickly grabbed her kids and left the house, forgetting that she had lasagna baking in the oven.

Several hours later, her phone rang again while she was in the waiting room of the hospital. This time it was her neighbor asking if she was home, because the smoke alarm had been going off continuously in her house. Her husband was being wheeled in for emergency surgery, but Timmi had to rush home to deal with the alarm.

Opening the front door, she was greeted with black, billowing smoke from her now burned lasagna. She began frantically opening windows, and almost slipped on a pool of water on the floor. There was a leak coming from the laundry room!

She stopped in her tracks and yelled at the top of her lungs, *"God, what have I done to deserve this?!"* Had God given her more than she could handle? The next night, her question was answered.

Timmi and I were invited to a Catholic church to hear a woman named Immaculée Ilibagiza share her story of faith. During the genocide in Rwanda in 1994, she had lost her entire family, except for one brother who was studying out of the country. For 91 days, she lived in hiding with seven other women in a bathroom no larger than 12 square feet. Her days were filled with the fear of being discovered. She remained in a state of constant prayer, reading the Bible and praying with her rosary from the moment she woke up until the moment she fell asleep at night.

When she was finally able to escape, Immaculée encountered a man with a machete who threatened to kill her. She stared him down, and miraculously her energy caused him to spare her life. At another time, she came face-to-face with the man who had murdered her mother and brother. Rather than lash out or run in fear, she said, "I forgive you." Immaculée credits her faith for her ability to handle these two situations with such strength and grace.

Her tragic story touched the heart of every person in the church. Timmi looked at me with tears in her eyes and whispered, "I just realized that my faith isn't as strong as I thought it was." At that moment, Timmi knew in her heart that in order to get through the ups and downs of her own life, she needed a daily practice of prayer.

PRAYER AND MIRACLES
MEDITATION RITUAL

TIME FRAME: *22 minutes daily*

You may be asking yourself: *Are prayer and meditation the same?* According to most major religions, the reason we're here on Earth is to work toward the perfection of the soul. Thus the question becomes, how can we perfect our soul and understand life in the greatest way possible? For some, it isn't about calming the mind, but being in a place of quiet contemplation with prayer. For others, it's about the breath and letting thoughts fade away.

For me, meditation and prayer are two different ways of attaining the same results—being centered, finding clarity, and having a deeper connection to a higher power.

That said, many people use prayer as their preferred form of meditation. For some, it's God's prescription. Mindful meditation through prayer renders the best results when practiced on a daily basis for 40 days.

As we've mentioned, it takes 40 days to change a habit and to retrain the mind and nervous system. The time you devote to your practice may be 10 minutes, 30 minutes, or longer, but it should be for at least 40 days.

The most important part of this ritual is consistency. If you can't be consistent with yourself, how can you be consistent with anything else?

WHAT YOU'LL NEED:

---

2 Clear Quartz spheres to be held in your hands to help you focus more clearly and enter a deeper state of meditation

1 meditation pillow or a comfortable chair

1 picture that represents who you are praying or devoting the meditation to

1 white candle as a symbolic way of letting spirit know you're connecting

1 Palo Santo wood stick to keep the energy grounded and clear while bringing blessings into your space

A timer

1 sage stick

1 feather

1 abalone shell or fireproof container to catch ashes from the sage

RITUAL STEPS:

1. Sage your environment, and cleanse your crystals (page 22).

2. Sit in a comfortable cross-legged position on the floor with a meditation pillow or in a chair with your feet firmly planted on the ground.

3. Hold your Clear Quartz spheres in your hands, close your eyes, and take 3 deep breaths. Aloud or in your head, say the following: *"I ask that the highest vibration of love and light connect with my highest self to clear all unwanted energy and any previous programming. I command these crystals to hold the intention that my prayers be answered and for miracles to come into my life. Thank you, thank you, thank you."*

4. Put your Clear Quartz spheres to the side and light your white candle.

5. Burn the Palo Santo, letting the scent fill the air. This infuses your space with blessings.

6. With your chosen picture in front of you, deepen your meditation by dedicating your practice to that someone or something. (In this particular ritual, meditation and prayer are interchangeable.) This dedication can be said internally or stated aloud.

7. Connect with your faith or spiritual practice by chanting or praying, or in some other way you prefer. Set the timer for 11 minutes.

8. Close your eyes and take 3 deep breaths in through the nose and out through the mouth. Begin your chanting, praying, or way of connecting with your faith. After the timer goes off, open your eyes and gently reacclimate to your surroundings. Then set the timer for 11 minutes again.

9. Place a Clear Quartz sphere in each of your hands, and hold them throughout the remainder of the meditation. Having the crystals in your hands will bring you clarity. If you become distracted and your thoughts begin to wander, focus on the crystals. Feel their weight and energy, and use them as an anchor to shift your focus back to your meditation.

10. Take 3 deep breaths in through your nose, exhaling through your mouth. This will set the stage for your meditation to begin.

11. Practice deep, rhythmic breathing throughout the 11 minutes.

12. When you're finished, take a moment to give thanks for your practice. End your meditation by bowing down with your hands at your heart in prayer. Say "amen," "thank you," or "namaste" 3 times. By repeating any of these words 3 times, you solidify their energy.

13. Now give thanks to yourself for taking the time to fill up your "spiritual gas tank." By doing so, you'll spread this energy of gratitude throughout your day, and it will affect everyone you meet.

14. Repeat steps 1 through 13 as often as needed.

COLOR ME PRETTY

Meditation can take many forms—prayer, walking in nature, or even washing the dishes. In fact, any activity can be a form of meditation if it is done with a conscious focus.

Coloring can be an easy form of meditation. It allows you to connect with your inner child—the creative, open-minded, playful, and free-spirited part of you that often gets overlooked. Coloring also helps you organize your thoughts and focus on the task at hand, which encourages relaxation.

The simple act of coloring forces you to focus on using your hands and eyes together, effectively eliminating the ability to multitask. After all, you can't be typing on your computer or tablet while you're coloring in patterns.

Clear Quartz

WISDOM KEEPER:
CRYSTAL CLEAR

COLOR: Clear, colorless, transparent to translucent

ORIGIN: Found worldwide but mostly in Brazil, India, and the U.S.

HISTORY AND LORE: The Quartz family is full of high-frequency overachievers. Keeping up with the Quartzes can be like keeping up with the Joneses—it's hard to match its universal power.

One of the most iconic crystals, it's also one of the most common. Clear Quartz, made up of silicon dioxide, can be found in every continent on Earth. Many of the ancient cultures from around the world have their own Clear Quartz myths. In the Middle Ages, Clear Quartz crystal balls were said to give clairvoyants amplified ability to predict the future. Native South American cultures believed the icy transparency of Clear Quartz crystals carved into skulls held the spirits of their ancestors. Ancient Japanese myths regarded Clear Quartz as a crystal of purification and endurance.

HEALING PROPERTIES: Clear Quartz may be a rock star among crystals, but it's no diva—it shares its spotlight. For those whose spirit needs illumination, clear quartz brings clarity to shadows within the mind. The reason there is so much lore surrounding it is because of how intensely it resonates with the body. A universal healer, it links to all chakras to provide balance and harmony. Its ability to be programmed for manifestation is unlike any other crystal. Clear Quartz is even used in electronics due to its ability to amplify and be programmed. If it works for your cell phone, imagine what it can do for your overall energy. By elevating thoughts and perspective, it will be able to manifest your intentions like never before.

MEDITATIVE COLORING RITUAL

WHAT YOU'LL NEED:

A copy of page 53 or a coloring book

Colored pencils, markers, or crayons

1 Flame Aura Quartz crystal to open yourself up to the full color spectrum

RITUAL STEPS:

1. Gather your coloring supplies, crystal, and copy of page 53 or coloring book.
2. Hold your Flame Aura Quartz crystal in your hands. Take 3 deep breaths, and feel your stress begin to melt away.
3. Place your crystal next to your paper. Your meditative coloring begins when your pen, pencil, or crayon touches the paper.
4. As you color, visualize your stress, anxiety, and negative emotions being replaced with color and happiness. Enjoy!

REDUCE ANXIETY WITH
A GROUP MEDITATION RITUAL

TIME FRAME: *11 minutes*

When you're feeling anxious and your heart is racing, gather a few friends, and sit together in silence for 11 minutes. This simple meditation will harmonize your breath and allow peace to outweigh any anxiety, worry, stress, fear, or uncertainty.

WHAT YOU'LL NEED:

A few friends—from 2 to 200

1 large Labradorite crystal to align you with the energy of the universe

A timer

1 sage stick

1 feather

1 abalone shell or fireproof container to catch ashes from the sage

RITUAL STEPS:

1. Sage your environment, and cleanse your crystals (page 22).
2. Choose 1 person to program the Labradorite crystal. Have this person hold the crystal in their hands, close their eyes, and take 3 deep breaths. Aloud or in their head, have them say the following: *"I ask that the highest vibration of love and light connect with my highest self to clear all unwanted energy and any previous programming. I command this crystal to hold the intention of reducing anxiety and bringing harmony to myself and everyone in this group. Thank you, thank you, thank you."*
3. Ask everyone to sit cross-legged in a circle. If you only have 2 people, sit across from each other. Try to touch knees, if possible, so that you stay connected to one another.
4. Place the Labradorite crystal in the middle of the group (or between you if only 2 people).

5. Set your timer for 11 minutes.
6. Close your eyes, and take 3 deep breaths, in through your nose and out through your mouth.
7. For the remainder of the time, just be. Experience the present moment with the people around you.
8. When the timer goes off, gently open your eyes, and notice how you feel. Do you feel less anxious than you did 11 minutes ago?

"The mistake new meditators often make is to look for signs of success within the meditation itself. . . . True success can only be determined by what happens outside of your daily practice."

— LIGHT WATKINS,
meditation practitioner and author

CHAPTER 5

THE TEMPLE WITHIN

3 STEPS TO GETTING TO KNOW YOURSELF THROUGH SELF-REFLECTION AND INNER TRANSFORMATION

"The journey of self is to be aware of self and understand the path which lies ahead is only laid out for you to learn to love and accept yourself."

— SHAMAN DUREK,
third generation shaman, spiritual guide, and healer

I T WAS ANOTHER PICTURE-PERFECT DAY IN SOUTHERN CALIFORNIA, AND I WAS SHOWING A REAL ESTATE CLIENT ONE OF THE MOST BEAUTIFUL BEACHFRONT mansions in Manhattan Beach. As we looked out the window at the waves breaking on the shore, he said, "This is what I've always wanted."

His clarity was inspiring, and I wanted that, too. I looked at him, smiling, and thought, *This is what I thought I wanted, but not anymore. I'm going to stop selling real estate.* It wasn't exactly a sudden revelation; the thought had been on my mind for at least a year.

On the outside, I had it all. I was young, healthy, and making a great living, with amazing family members and friends by my side. But I felt empty.

It was the invisible things that were consuming my mind. The things we can't go out

and purchase—peace, contentment, fulfillment, and inner silence. Don't get me wrong: selling real estate was good to me. But over time, my passion for it began to wane. Something deep within my heart kept urging me to open up and meet the "real" me, but I had no idea how to find her. *Maybe I should go to India, I thought, and meet a spiritual guru, or travel to the Amazon to study with an indigenous shaman to learn about plant medicine. Or maybe I could start over again in a new state.*

I mentioned these ideas to one of my astrologer friends, who asked, "Why do you always have to be such a Scorpio extremist? Does it always have to be all or nothing?" Yes. To me, it usually did. She then explained that one of the reasons I was questioning my life at 29 years of age was because I was going through a *Saturn Return.*

The planet Saturn is the cosmic taskmaster, similar to a very demanding, disciplined teacher who holds us accountable. In more technical terms, Saturn takes 29.7 Earth years to orbit the Sun and return to the same zodiac sign it was in when you were born. So this time period in your life acts as a rite of passage, bringing you face-to-face with your fears, while at the same time demanding that you evaluate what's important. You're given the opportunity to overcome obstacles and to gain the wisdom that you'll need to reach your highest potential.

I must have had a terrified look on my face because my friend quickly added, "Look at it as an initiation into adulthood. You're being given the gift of finding out who you truly are."

My 20s felt like I had been living in a masquerade ball. I wore different "costumes" based on my career choices, my boyfriends and friends, and what I did for fun. Each time I put on a new costume, I played a different role. Some days I might be "adulting," while other days I might be a carefree artist or beach girl. Of course, it's socially acceptable to be curious in one's 20s. It's the time to try new things, party into the wee hours, and be anything *but* settled down. But it all seemed to change when I turned 29. Suddenly, "When are you going to settle down, get married, and have babies?" was the new question.

I wanted to say, "Well, here's the thing: my new life coach is a planet called Saturn, and Saturn's job is to kick my ass so that I finally learn who I am! How can you ask me about marriage and babies at a time like this?"

For the first time in my life, my mortality hit me like a bolt of lightning. It was frightening. I felt overwhelmed. I wanted to throw my "real estate agent" costume out the window and run far away. But even then, I knew that no matter how far I ran, it wouldn't change who I was. My external environment wasn't going to solve my internal conflict.

There was only one place to go, and that was within. It was the scariest place of all because there, I wouldn't be needing a costume. In fact, I'd be maybe even a little naked! I had no idea where to start.

Eventually, I discovered what I've come to call my "temple within," where my true self resides. Working with crystals helped me get there.

What about you? Have you visited that temple? Maybe you remember your own Saturn Return, or you're experiencing it right now. Wherever you are and whatever you're experiencing, connecting with your inner temple is one of the most profound steps you can take to find your authenticity. And you'll find that the crystals are waiting to help you, as they were for me.

In the rituals to come, you will be taken through three steps—inner reflection, embracing your light and shadow sides, and letting go of control—to bring you closer to finding your temple within.

STEP 1:
INNER REFLECTION

The first step to finding the temple within is to see yourself for who you truly are, without judgment, and with wholehearted acceptance.

To do this, it's important to make the time and space for the real you to come forth in your life.

This isn't a quick fix! It's important to make a daily, conscious effort to be aware, honest, and open about the new spiritual lifestyle you're undertaking.

Black Obsidian

WISDOM KEEPER:
THE MIRROR

COLOR: Black

ORIGIN: Found in many locations, including Europe, Japan, South America, and the U.S.

HISTORY AND LORE: Mirror, mirror, on the wall, who is the most self-aware of them all? With this stone in hand, it's probably you. Black Obsidian has long been touted for its metaphysical abilities and historically significant uses. This structureless rock is also known as volcanic glass because of its smooth, reflective luster. This stone forms when lava cools too rapidly to form crystalline structures. In the Stone Age, civilizations around the world used Obsidian to create arrowheads, spears, and cutting tools. While still used as a cutting tool in some modern-day industries, Obsidian is more useful on a personal level. It will help you to emotionally slice away negative energy.

HEALING PROPERTIES: Facing the good, the bad, and the ugly parts of ourselves is hard, but Obsidian makes it easier. By showing you a reflection of your true self, Obsidian forces you to accept yourself entirely. It connects to the root chakra to ground you during contemplation. Working with Black Obsidian will assist you in cutting the stress and negative patterns from your life by first bringing them to your attention. As you see what needs to be expelled from your life, Obsidian rewards you by absorbing that toxic energy. No wonder it's called the stone of truth!

INNER REFLECTION RITUAL

TIME FRAME: *11 minutes daily for 21 days*

The Inner Reflection Ritual encourages you to check in with your thoughts, feelings, and emotions, allowing them to come to the surface instead of covering them up or pushing them away. As you gaze at your reflection on the surface of a piece of Obsidian—a volcanic glass rock—you can see that happiness and fulfillment don't exist outside of you, but within you. And you have both of them by choice, not happenstance. Going to your temple within allows you the time you'll need to transform your life. It gives you a safe space where you can shift the habits, beliefs, and thoughts that have kept you stuck in old patterns.

WHAT YOU'LL NEED:

1 flat Black Obsidian stone to act as an "Obsidian mirror" to gaze into

A timer

1 sage stick

1 feather

1 abalone shell or fireproof container to catch ashes from the sage

RITUAL STEPS:

1. Sage your environment, and cleanse your crystals (page 22).
2. Hold the Black Obsidian crystal in your hands, close your eyes, and take 3 deep breaths. Aloud or in your head, say the following: *"I ask that the highest vibration of love and light connect with my highest self to clear all unwanted energy and any previous programming. I command this crystal to hold the intention of reflection, transformation, and acceptance. Thank you, thank you, thank you."*
3. Set the timer for 11 minutes.
4. Hold the Obsidian in your hands, and take 7 long, deep breaths in and out. Gaze into the Obsidian mirror, and see your reflection on its surface. Now look deeper into your own eyes. Without judging, what do you see? Observe your thoughts as they come up, but try to simply be a witness to these thoughts without judging them. See if you can go deeper into your eyes and see the self

behind the self. As images or thoughts come up, observe them as if they're pictures on a screen that just pass by. Continue to breathe deeply. As you allow images, thoughts, and feelings to surface, keep looking into the Obsidian mirror. Breathe deeply with the intention of inhaling transformation and healing into every cell of your being.

5. Once you've had time to sit with your thoughts, send love to your reflection. Then send forgiveness and, finally, send thanks to your reflection. Every time your mind wanders, look in the Obsidian mirror, and love yourself even more. Focus on the truth of your past and the love of the self that exists right now.

6. After your 11 minutes are complete, place your Obsidian mirror on your bedside table to hold the space of reflection, transformation, and acceptance as you continue to work through this process.

7. Every day for 21 days, repeat steps 2 through 6. Look in the Obsidian mirror, love yourself, and give thanks for all the lessons in your life. They have made you the person you are today.

STEP 2:
FROM BAR TO TEMPLE

The second step to discovering your true self and finding the temple within is admitting that there are multiple sides that make up the whole of who you are. You don't have to act in only one way to be on a spiritual path.

For this section of the chapter, let's define the word *temple* as your light side, which represents the way you feed your physical, mental, and spiritual bodies in positive and fulfilling ways. It's what you choose to embrace in yourself.

On the other side is the "bar." Let's define this as your shadow or dark side, which includes negative thinking, limiting beliefs, old patterns, bad habits, overindulgences, and addictions. It's what you choose to overlook or deny. (By no means are we saying that a temple is "good" and a bar is "bad"; they're simply part of this metaphor.)

Both of these sides affect how your interior and exterior selves look and feel. If you're completely honest with yourself, you'll know when your internal bar and temple are out of balance. When you go inward and connect to a higher power (whatever that means for you), you're aligned with your personal truth. Hopefully you'll have the desire, motivation, and willingness to spend the majority of your time in the temple. But there's always an underlying and constant temptation drawing you to the bar.

Being on a spiritual journey to self-discovery isn't always filled with light. Finding who

you truly are on a soul level doesn't happen overnight—it takes time and dedication. With the dark comes light and vice versa. Some days you might find yourself in the temple, some days in the bar, and other days might be a combination of both.

There are several important things to remember while you're finding the balance between your inner bar and temple:

- Don't beat yourself up if you find yourself at the bar. Don't stop showing up at the temple because you feel you're not living up to the so-called image of spirituality or positivity.

- The journey is different for everyone, and there's no right or wrong way to get there. Please don't try to compare yourself to anyone else, because everyone evolves and grows at a different pace.

- When you're on the spiritual path, it's easy to judge others for not being on "your level." You may find that the people surrounding you don't understand your new path. Remember that others find themselves and their own paths at different times. If someone's lifestyle choices don't parallel yours, that's okay. Don't judge them for it, just as you wouldn't want them to judge you.

- The important part is showing up for yourself on a daily basis and trusting that you're on the right path. The journey within is not about perfection; it's about consistency.

Every day that you chip away at what holds you back from embracing your true self is another day that you come closer to your temple within. Taking time to shift your focus from the outside world to your personal journey inward is the fastest way to transformation.

EMBRACING THE LIGHT
AND SHADOW WITHIN RITUAL

TIME FRAME: *Once a week for 4 weeks*

Once you accept that your light and shadow sides are both parts of who you are, you can begin to heal from the inside out and find your true self. This ritual can be used to examine your light side (temple) or your shadow side (bar), and then find neutrality between them.

You'll make a list of all the things in your life that constitute your light side—what you like about being you. This list is a visual reminder for you to respect and honor the characteristics that make you magnificent.

The next list you'll make consists of the things you want to work on within yourself—your shadow side. It's meant for honest self-reflection, not self-loathing. Everyone has lessons to work on in life. That's our job as humans!

The third list you'll make will allow you to look at both your light and shadow characteristics, and think about what can be shifted to bring more balance into your life.

You always have the choice to evolve. You decide which parts of yourself you want to feed, and which parts you want to face head-on and conquer. Know that it will be a lifelong, ever-evolving journey to balance your light and shadow sides.

WHAT YOU'LL NEED:

1 Zebra Jasper crystal, which carries a balanced energy; the white and black represents the light and the shadow (or yin and yang energy) coexisting

1 journal or 3 blank pieces of white paper

1 blue pen—blue is the color of truth. It's believed that you're more likely to retain information when you write it with blue ink.

1 sage stick

1 feather

1 abalone shell or fireproof container to catch ashes from the sage

RITUAL STEPS:

1. Sage your environment, and cleanse your crystals (page 22).
2. Hold the Zebra Jasper crystal in your hands, close your eyes, and take 3 deep breaths. Aloud or in your head, say the following: *"I ask that the highest vibration of love and light connect with my highest self to clear all unwanted energy and any previous programming. I command this crystal to hold the intention of truth, objectivity, and neutrality. Thank you, thank you, thank you."*
3. Hold the Zebra Jasper crystal in your nonwriting hand. Look at the swirling pattern of black and white. Notice how the colors coexist, mirroring how the light and shadow exist within you. While looking at the crystal, start to make a "light list" with your other hand of all the things that represent the light within you.
4. Make a "shadow list" of all the things that you would like to work on within yourself.
5. Look at your light and shadow lists, and reflect on how you can shift to achieve more neutrality within yourself.
6. Make a third list of what you can do that will bring more balance into your life so that it isn't always black or white.
7. Once a week for 4 weeks, repeat steps 2 through 6.
8. At the end of 4 weeks, compare the data you compiled about yourself. See if your lists have evolved from week 1 to 4.
9. Keep the crystal in a place where you can see it or hold it whenever you want. Your crystal is a symbolic reminder of the balance you wish to hold within yourself.

STEP 3:
LETTING GO OF CONTROL

The third and final step to discovering your true self and finding the temple within is letting go of control. When you let go of trying to control everything, you create the necessary space needed to bring in what you want in your life. By trying to constantly control everything, the energy stops and you become stuck, blocked, and stagnant. When you surrender the control, you're able to see all the opportunities that are continually around you. For Timmi, and many others, this step is a work in progress that is continuously revisited.

Timmi has always been very efficient with her time. As an only child, she learned how to be organized and self-sufficient at a young age. Without siblings to hide behind or blend in with, all the attention was on her all the time. She grew up with a strong desire to please her parents and grandparents, and as a result, she put enormous pressure on herself to be perfect.

To this day, Timmi maximizes every minute of every hour. It's safe to say she gets more done in a 24-hour period than most people do in a week. I have my suspicions. I beg her to admit she's actually an alien, or at least a robot. It's the only way her efficiency could make sense.

Timmi aims to be prepared for every situation. She is constantly thinking ahead and always has a "just in case" scenario at the ready. Whenever she finds herself with a moment of free time, she'll voice-log data, memories, notes, pictures, and contact information into her phone for future reference. She's a walking historian of her life. Maybe this is a Gemini thing? (Since Geminis are known to have two personalities—two people for the price of one—they are known to be doubly prepared.) If I forget something that happened in our past, all I have to do is reference the month and year, and Timmi will pull up her notes and remind me. (I must say her habit came in extremely handy while writing this book.)

Timmi's grandpa, whom she adored, would often tell her that she needed to slow down, stop, and smell the roses. He was a happy and gregarious Italian man who was full of life and always had an insightful message to share. "You're right," she'd tell him, giving him a quick peck on the cheek. But then she'd run out the door and get back to doing whatever was next on her (endless) to-do list.

When her grandpa passed away a couple of years ago, Timmi was devastated. It happened unexpectedly. While cleaning out his personal belongings, his family discovered a box full of white napkins. On each napkin, Timmi's grandfather had written messages and phrases. It was as if he wanted these nuggets of wisdom to be found after his death, so he would always be remembered. Seven hundred napkins were found, but only one of them had a message that was directed to a specific person—and that was to Timmi. The napkin read: "Chaotic, that's Timmi."

She was stunned. How could the man she adored, respected, and looked up to have written such a thing about her? At first she was angry. How could he possibly think someone so über-organized and efficient was chaotic?

Timmi's life moved forward, but her grandfather's words continued to haunt her. She began to notice that when she looked at her life from a macro perspective, it was a well-oiled, efficient

machine. But when she looked at it from a micro perspective, her hyper-control did indeed create chaos. Why? Because life is full of unexpected twists and turns, and whenever something happened that she hadn't anticipated, she would be derailed. It would thrust her out of her comfort zone and into—you guessed it—chaos.

In the end, Timmi's grandfather gave her the biggest gift of all—the truth. With it came an opportunity for her to look at herself in a new way.

During this same period, there were other parts of Timmi's life that began spinning out of control. She had listed her house for sale but reconsidered and decided to take it off the market. As soon as she did, she got an offer with a request for a 30-day escrow. At the same time, her teenage son was going through a difficult time and needed 100 percent of her attention. Everything was happening too fast and all at once. There was no way for her to control any of it. In fact, for the first time, she realized she wasn't in control—at all. The only choice she had was to surrender, and it was terrifying. But she understood that this was her wake-up call; she needed to find her temple within. She needed to listen to the voice inside of her that said, *It's time to focus on me.*

Letting go and surrendering to upheaval take bravery and courage. It's hard to be honest with yourself—to see the good, the bad, and the ugly. But by doing so, you can finally begin to let go of self-imposed limitations and the habits that are in the way of true fulfillment.

LETTING GO +
SURRENDERING RITUAL

TIME FRAME:
11 minutes a day for 3 consecutive days

This ritual enlists the energy of Mother Earth to help you let go, surrender, and allow the Earth to absorb any unwanted energy. It will help you ground yourself back into your body. When you're grounded and connected to the Earth and your body, you can make better decisions and tap into your inner truth. In this space, you can determine what no longer serves you and discover what you need to feel balanced.

We connect to the Earth through our feet. When you place your feet firmly upon the grounding crystals, they act as a very gentle reflexology massage. This stimulates your body's healing process and helps to bring your body into a state of deep relaxation.

As you place your feet on the crystals, visualize stuck, negative, and unwanted energy leaving through the soles of your feet to be absorbed into the Earth. This is a way to energetically let go of what holds you back from moving forward in life. This ritual can help you become more mindful of staying grounded and connected to the temple within.

WHAT YOU'LL NEED:

9 Basalt stones to create a shift in your life and release old patterns

10 Black Obsidian stones for cleansing, drawing out mental stress and tension, and providing protection

4 Hematite stones for grounding, balance, and absorbing negativity

1 tub or bucket that is large enough to soak your feet

1 cup of Epsom salts

1 pitcher to hold warm water

1 towel

A timer

1 sage stick

1 feather

1 abalone shell or fireproof container to catch ashes from the sage

RITUAL STEPS:

1. Sage your environment, and cleanse your crystals (page 22).
2. Place all the crystals in one area. Aloud or in your head, say the following:
   "I ask that the highest vibration of love and light connect with my highest self to clear all unwanted energy and any previous programming. I command these crystals to hold the intention of releasing negativity and old patterns, grounding, and balance. Thank you, thank you, thank you."
3. Find a place where you can relax comfortably while soaking your feet. Place a towel on the ground with the tub (or bucket) on top of it.
4. Place all the crystals and 1 cup of Epsom salts in the tub.

5. Fill the pitcher with warm water, and pour enough into the tub so that it will cover your feet.

6. Before you place your feet in the tub, take 3 deep breaths. Breathe in light, and breathe out any negative thoughts.

7. Place your feet in the tub.

8. Set the timer for 11 minutes.

9. As you sit in stillness, feel the crystals grounding your energy field. Feel your mind, body, and spirit reconnecting with each other and becoming one.

10. Visualize your feet plugging into the energy of the Earth. Feel yourself releasing, letting go, and surrendering through the soles of your feet anything that no longer serves your highest good.

11. As your breath and body begin to stabilize, feel the peace, connection, and harmony that reside within you.

12. When you're finished, remove the crystals, dump the water into the toilet, and flush it away.

13. Practice steps 1 through 12 for 3 consecutive days.

Basalt

FIND THE FIRE WITHIN

COLOR: Dark gray to black

ORIGIN: Found in many locations, including Iceland, India, South Africa, and the U.S.

HISTORY AND LORE: Basalt has the ultimate before-and-after transformation story. Once, it was volcanic magma, leading a tumultuous and never stationary life. As it rose toward the surface, its fiery disposition cooled, and it became a source of solidity and support for much of the Earth's surface and ocean basins. For centuries, Basalt has been used in a variety of ways, from decorative to curative. In ancient Rome, the natural durability and hardness of Basalt made it the optimal choice for paving roads. Ancient Egyptians, however, used this black stone for carving immense statues. Today it's used in spas for hot stone treatments.

HEALING PROPERTIES: Basalt's energy is both intense and soothing. As an energetically absorbent stone, it removes negative energy and stagnant emotions that block your good energy from circulating. It is thought of as a stone of courage and stability. During difficult transitions, Basalt provides confidence and support. It is used in therapeutic hot stone massages to take away pain while providing nurturing warmth for healing.

The spiritual journey takes a lot of work, and nobody can do it for you. It's up to you to put in the effort. The journey to find the temple within begins at a different time for everyone. For me, it was when I was 29, and for Timmi, it was when she turned 47. There's no right or wrong time for it to start, just as there's no such thing as being "late."

How will you know when it's time for you? Your old way of living will no longer feel enough. Even the unknown will begin to feel better than the known. For the first time in your life, you'll feel an irresistible urge to find out who you are on a deeper level.

You'll realize that self-reflection will help you choose truth, self-love, and acceptance.

"If you don't have any shadows, you're not standing in the light."

— LADY GAGA,
pop singer and songwriter

CHAPTER 6

BE A MONEY MAGNET

HOW TO ATTRACT PROSPERITY, SUCCESS, AND ABUNDANCE

"What matters is that you master money and it doesn't master you. Then you are free to live life on your own terms."

— TONY ROBBINS,
life and business strategist, entrepreneur, best-selling author, and philanthropist

OUR BUSINESS STARTED OUT OF THE TRUNKS OF OUR CARS IN MANHATTAN BEACH, CALIFORNIA. WE WERE KNOWN around town as the "flip-flop girls" who sold "energy beads" because, early on, we did business in our flip-flops and yoga clothes. I wish I could say that we had a business plan or even a master plan. We didn't. What we did have, however, was an optimistic attitude, a gold-mine idea, and crystals around our necks.

I had used the money I made in real estate to study with healers, medicine people, and indigenous experts from different parts of the world. This allowed me to travel the globe and explore to my heart's content. When I returned home, I began to discover yoga, meditation, chanting, and crystals.

I was feeling the love, but sadly, my savings account was not. It was time to figure out what I was going to do for a living.

I needed a reality check, so I asked my mom for ideas. She paused and said with her quick Irish wit, "Heather, you're standing by the side of the road, starving to death with a loaf of bread in your hands. You have all this information on energy and healing. Do something with it!"

She was right! It was time to attract money into my life, so I combined my knowledge of Feng Shui with my love of crystals and jewelry. As a result, the Prosperity Necklace was born. It was energy technology for the mind, body, and spirit.

The secret formula consisted of three Chinese coins tied together with red thread, combined with a string of jade beads, which are known to bring prosperity. My definition of prosperity expanded beyond money. I saw it as opportunity for new doors to open and new

Heather (left) and Timmi (right) packing up orders of Prosperity necklaces.

connections to be made with people who would enrich my life.

Prosperity can be a process, but I had to put a timeline on this experiment to see if my formula worked. I made 10 Prosperity Necklaces, gave them to 10 people, and asked them to let me know in 10 days if any shifts in prosperity had happened. Keep in mind that I gave the necklaces to my 10 *most skeptical friends*—the ones who were "very concerned" about this new path I had chosen.

"You want me to wear these crystals?" they'd ask.

"Yes. For ten days."

"Why?"

"To see if wearing the energy of the Earth on your body as a talisman will remind you of your intention in regard to prosperity."

"Huh?"

"Just wear it. Please."

At this point, Timmi—who knew me better than myself sometimes—had seen me go through plenty of "phases" before, but something about this time was different. She wanted to know what I was up to. She wondered why I would leave a good income and a solid career to travel to remote jungles in search of my "spirit." She could see that my travels had changed me. She was intrigued—and brave. She agreed to be one of my guinea pigs.

So, what happened? All 10 people came back after 10 days reporting an increase in prosperity. The necklace had worked! Some received unexpected money in the mail, some had been given new opportunities, and some had even been surprised with a raise. Word spread like wildfire. All around our little beach town, people wanted to know about this Prosperity Necklace. The original 10 people told 10 people, who told 10 people, and so on, and so on. And just like that, my business was off to a *prosperous* start!

But I had a problem: I didn't know how to produce the product. This is where Timmi, my lifelong best friend, entered the picture. She knew how to get things made. She had been in the garment industry for 12 years, selling women's clothing to mass-market retailers. It was a competitive and grueling job, and she had become so burned out that she'd recently walked away from it. She agreed to help me. So within a week, production of the Prosperity Necklace began in earnest.

Orders were coming in so quickly that the minute we had them made, cleansed, and energized, we filled the trunks of our cars and personally delivered them. It didn't take long for the Hollywood A-listers to hear about the energy beads from the flip-flop girls in Manhattan Beach—which is only a few miles away from La La Land.

Soon, we were ushered into exclusive Hollywood parties, where we were placed in back rooms to sell our crystal beads to the rich and famous. It was as if we were energy dealers, supplying the elite with a secret competitive edge. Meanwhile, the necklace was working for us, too. It was raining money as we rubbed elbows with some of the most prosperous people in the world.

As our business grew, we found an office with an ocean view in Manhattan Beach and hired employees. But in order to keep up with the demand, we had to find capital to expand. That's when we were officially in business.

Let me add here that Timmi and I could write an entire book on what *not* to do in business. We've made every mistake imaginable, but we've always listened to our intuition and asked for help. Two decades later, we're still surrounding ourselves with smart, resourceful people—and always *the energy of the crystals.*

Heather and Timmi doing crystal energy readings backstage at a private event.

CRYSTAL CLARITY

Looking back now, the fact that our business was so easy for us at the beginning was more a curse than a blessing. When things flowed effortlessly, we forgot a very important universal law: *gratitude*. We took for granted all the blessings that came our way, and eventually we were taught a hard lesson. We were reminded

---

TIPS TO BOOST YOUR PROSPERITY

- Never put your purse on the ground, as that will drain your money energy.

- Rub elbows with someone who is prosperous, and their luck will rub off on you.

- Wear Tiger's Eye, Jade, Aventurine, or Pyrite on your body to attract wealth.

- Clogged or leaking plumbing equals clogged or leaking finances. Fix any plumbing issues immediately!

- Keep bathroom doors shut and the lid to the toilet seat down at all times because it prevents loss of energy and money.

- To keep money flowing, place a piece of Citrine in the cash register of your business.

- Carry a $100 bill hidden in your wallet so that you always feel abundant.

---

very quickly that this new business was not about us, our egos, or the "cool people" we met. Our success was never really about us—it was *always* about the crystals.

"Those girls are so consumed with the business that they've forgotten what's at the heart of it. Us!" This is what the crystals seemed to suddenly say to us. "It's time to show them our quiet stillness so that they know who we are."

Yikes.

Over the next few months, our business slowed drastically. The initial hype of the Prosperity Necklace died down. We heard the crystals' "quiet" message loud and clear. We were forced to stop the business entirely while we tried to develop other products that could be just as powerful as the Prosperity Necklace. Unfortunately, our minds were clouded with the fear of the unknown. The crystals, with their infinite wisdom, watched us spiral downward.

Finally, one day we decided to lie on the floor with stones on every part of our bodies. They were everywhere! Black Tourmaline between the feet, Hematite on the root chakra, Carnelian on the second chakra, Pyrite over the third chakra, Rose Quartz on the heart, Turquoise on the throat, Amethyst over our third eye chakra, and Clear Quartz crystal points all around us. We lay there for hours, sometimes in complete silence and sometimes talking through our fears.

Slowly, our energetic bodies settled back into our physical bodies. As our minds started to open up and the fear dissolved back into the Earth, everything became crystal clear. It was time to start over. We needed a new plan of action because the old ways were no longer working.

CULTIVATING SPIRITUAL WEALTH

Those "old ways" had a lot to do with our mind-set. You see, at the start of our business, Timmi and I often found ourselves conflicted about how being "spiritual" and "material" could coexist. On a deep subconscious level, we didn't believe they could, which is why we often found ourselves in financial trouble.

We believed that healers, who were of service to others, shouldn't make money. This mind-set almost cost us our business. And then we had an epiphany: With no money and no customers, there was no way we could be of service to anyone.

Spiritual wealth comes from within. It's your contentment, mindfulness, and spiritual self—and these are things that you can have at all times. True spiritual wealth is something that you can control, that no one can take from you. Material wealth often fluctuates. It is influenced not only by internal factors—such as poor financial decisions—but external factors as well, including the economy, natural disasters, and a host of other scenarios that are beyond your control.

The moment we consciously embraced the idea that material wealth can naturally flow out of spiritual wealth, our business shifted upward again. We created a wealth bowl, one that we keep in front of us on a daily basis, to keep us on track.

Tiger's Eye

WISDOM KEEPER:
SHAPE SHIFTER

COLOR: Yellow with golden brown stripes

ORIGIN: Found in many locations, including Australia, Brazil, South Africa, and the U.S.

HISTORY AND LORE: Tiger's Eye gets its name from its amber hues, but it is its ability to bestow fierce focus and primal power, just like that of a tiger, that gives the stone its real name. Another member of the renowned Quartz family, Tiger's Eye has been used for courage by warriors and soldiers since ancient times. Roman soldiers wore Tiger's Eye rings for strength and protection.

HEALING PROPERTIES: When you stare at a picture for too long, you start to lose clarity. The same thing happens with our perspective. When we look at a situation from one point of view for too long, our take on that situation becomes blurry. This crystal helps you see through a fresh set of eyes. Tiger's Eye brings your focus back by shifting your outlook. From this new point of view, you gain deeper understanding. Maybe it's time to explore a new hobby. Perhaps there's a solution to a business problem that you haven't yet considered. Using Tiger's Eye gets you out of your rut by showing you what changes you need to make. It connects to the solar plexus and sacral chakras, and helps ground the spirit. It can inspire you to find the courage needed to pursue new ventures.

SPIRITUAL WEALTH BOWL RITUAL

TIME FRAME: *40 days*

The Spiritual Wealth Bowl Ritual gives you an outlet to bring your thoughts and ideas into physical form. This small vessel—which represents your intentions, treasures, and goals—offers unlimited possibilities.

WHAT YOU'LL NEED:

A bowl to hold what represents your spiritual and material world. (Be creative! It can be a bowl, large clamshell, basket, fishbowl, glass candy jar, crystal vase, or similar.)

8 crystals—8 is the number of money. These crystals represent the gifts from the Earth. These can be any size, from tumbled stones to larger crystals:

- 1 Tiger's Eye, 1 Aventurine, 1 Citrine, and 1 Jade to represent material wealth

- 1 Amethyst, 1 Clear Quartz, 1 Labradorite, and 1 Dumortierite to represent spiritual wealth

7 wishes, goals, or intentions written on paper in blue ink. Be sure to write them in present tense!

Money—coins, bills, or currency from the countries where you would like to do business

A smiling, happy photo of you

Hard-copy images from magazines or the Internet that represent spirituality, contentment, mindfulness, and inner peace to you

Treasures that have meaning to you, such as a feather, shell, or gift from a loved one

Images of family members and friends who make you happy and with whom you want to share in your journey

Anything else that represents spiritual wealth to you

Something that's gold in color—coins, a painted rock, Pyrite crystal, a lucky Buddha, or similar

1 sage stick

1 feather

1 abalone shell or fireproof container to catch ashes from the sage

RITUAL STEPS:

1. Sage your environment, and cleanse your crystals (page 22).

2. Hold the crystals in your hands, close your eyes, and take 3 deep breaths. Aloud or in your head, say the following: *"I ask that the highest vibration of love and light connect with my highest self to clear all unwanted energy and any previous programming. I command these crystals to hold the intention of spiritual abundance and unlimited possibilities. Thank you. Thank you. Thank you."*

3. Find a place where your Spiritual Wealth Bowl can remain, somewhere you'll see it on a daily basis.

4. Place the crystals at the bottom of the bowl, and begin layering the other items on top of the crystals, reserving your gold item for the very top.

5. State your number 1 intention for your spiritual wealth out loud.

6. Leave your Spiritual Wealth Bowl in place for 40 days or until you feel a shift. Feel free to add to the bowl or "refresh" its energy by placing it out in the Sun.

SAY GOOD-BYE TO THE BLAMER AND COMPLAINER

Do you feel you've done everything you possibly can to change your financial situation, yet you keep getting the same result? Then, guess what? It's time to change your mind-set.

One of the biggest secrets to unlimited abundance is taking ownership of all that you feel, think, and believe, understanding that everything you have in life starts from within. This means that you stop blaming others for the problems in your life and stop complaining so much about those problems.

Knowing that it all starts with *you* gives you the power to make a choice. You can choose to live in a new state of happiness and abundance. The minute your brain grasps this concept, you're officially on the road to the life of your dreams.

Sadly, few people make this mind-set shift. Ironically, many are actually addicted to failure, disappointment, misery, and financial instability. It's true that feeling horrible about your financial situation is a tough habit to break. It isn't easy to be honest with yourself or to recognize how low you feel. So, too, if you take responsibility for your predicament, you'll now have to do something about it.

But take a breath and think about it. It really *is* good news that you have the power, the choice, and the tools within you to change your circumstances. These changes might not happen overnight, but we're living proof that with time and work, they can be done.

You have a choice: You can allow your mind to turn *against* you, or you can allow it to work *with* you. This is where the shift needs to happen.

Jade

WISDOM KEEPER:
LUCKY CHARM

COLOR: Green

ORIGIN: Found in many locations, including China, New Zealand, Canada, Mexico, and the U.S.

HISTORY AND LORE: Green Jade, known as Nephrite, is thought to be a secret good luck stone. For centuries, cultures all over the world have believed this stone brings good fortune. The Maori, an indigenous people of New Zealand, used Jade in talismans to guarantee long life. Aztecs and Mayans regarded Jade as a link to the gods, with the ability to cure kidney stones. Chinese lore held that Jade represented elements of virtue and happiness, like courage, purity, longevity, wealth, and wisdom.

HEALING PROPERTIES: Similar to ancient Chinese beliefs, this crystal is thought to bring good fortune into several areas of your life. As an element of the Earth, it makes you more open to prosperity and abundance. This abundance can come in the form of more than mere wealth. Whatever is in your heart, whether you are seeking enhancements in health, happiness, success, or relationships, Jade taps into an ancient dynasty of wisdom to guide you.

OWNERSHIP RITUAL

TIME FRAME: *7 days for 7 minutes a day*

Choose something in your life to take ownership of for the next 7 days. Shift your focus from "she," "he," and "they" and bring it back to "I." That's where the intention and the change happens—within yourself. Seeing your life from this perspective will not only put you in a position to change what's undesirable in your life, but will also help you own all the good things you've already created.

The magic in this Ownership Ritual is in taking responsibility for your situation without pointing fingers, blaming, complaining, or justifying. In 7 short days, not only will you start to own your true self again, but you'll see new ways to attract prosperity.

WHAT YOU'LL NEED:

A photo of yourself

7 Tectonic Quartz crystals—7 is the number for healing. The Tectonic Quartz is the result of a massive shift in energy from the Earth's movement, which caused the crystal to shift and shape into a new form.

1 small Clear Quartz point to activate your crystal grid

A timer

1 sage stick

1 feather

1 abalone shell or fireproof container to catch ashes from the sage

RITUAL STEPS:

1. Sage your environment, and cleanse your crystals (page 22).
2. Hold your Tectonic Quartz crystals in your hands, close your eyes, and take 3 deep breaths. Aloud or in your head, say the following: *"I ask that the highest vibration of love and light connect with my highest self to clear all unwanted energy and any previous programming. I command these crystals to hold the intention of movement, ownership, and financial abundance. Thank you, thank you, thank you."*

3. Place your photo on a table, the top of a bookshelf, a nightstand, or any area where it will be undisturbed and where you can see it on a daily basis.

4. Surround your photo with the 7 Tectonic Quartz crystals with the points directed inward. This is for inner reflection and helping you to make your own shift.

5. Activate your crystal grid with the Clear Quartz point. Starting from the outside, draw an invisible line between the stones to energetically connect each to the next. Think of it as "connecting the dots" like when you were a kid. A crystal grid is like a spiritual blueprint for your intention. It's a powerful tool for manifesting goals, desires, and intentions that unites the energies of the crystals, a sacred geometric pattern, and your intention. The combination of these three things helps to manifest results much faster.

6. Set the timer for 7 minutes. Gaze at your image. Ask yourself, *What needs to change in my financial life?* State your answers out loud. By saying them out loud, you're taking full ownership of why you're in your current situation without explaining, blaming, or complaining.

7. Look at this situation from a higher perspective. What are you accountable for? What was the lesson you were supposed to learn from any challenges you have faced? How can you do things differently in the future? How can you forgive yourself and others in regard to your finances so that you can move forward?

8. If old ways of thinking come up for you during this process, stop and take a few deep breaths. Calmly remind yourself that the old patterns didn't work. They kept you stuck, stagnant, and in a mind-set of lack. As you go within and own your life, you become empowered, free, and abundant.

9. Repeat steps 6 through 8 for 7 consecutive days.

BECOME A MONEY MAGNET

If you want to become a magnet for money, it's important to understand that money is a form of energy. Its true value is relative. One person might think a certain amount of money is a lot, while another person thinks the same amount is very little. So, it's important to ask yourself what value money holds for you. Of course, at different stages of your life, the value of money will shift and change.

I always find it interesting that people who are less affluent but have a strong connection to their family, community, and spirit seem to have the essence of happiness, which is true wealth. To have fulfillment and contentment in your financial life, you must identify what feeds you emotionally, spiritually, and mentally. How much money is truly necessary for you to create that fulfillment and contentment?

When you stay fluid, open-minded, and clear, the energy of money won't control you but will instead become a natural flow within your life. Someone who is a money magnet has a clear, balanced mind-set with a plan of action that holds their vision and values.

Aventurine

WISDOM KEEPER:

ODDS ARE IN YOUR
FAVOR TO MANIFEST
YOUR DREAMS

COLOR: Light to dark green

ORIGIN: Brazil, India, Russia, and Tanzania

HISTORY AND LORE: If you're heading to Las Vegas, forget about Lady Luck—Aventurine is what you want by your side! Known as the gambler's stone, the name Aventurine comes from the French word *aventure*, meaning "chance."

HEALING PROPERTIES: Many green stones are said to bring abundance, but the whimsical energy of this shimmering crystal is especially conducive to the power of plenty. While it's playfully referred to as a gambler's stone, Aventurine is helpful to everyone. Sometimes a gamble looks less like a game and more like a fork in the road of your life, a time when you have to decide between what is sound and secure or taking a risk. In connecting with the heart chakra, Aventurine graces the spirit with an easy sense of confidence. The excitement it stimulates can promote a more optimistic outlook that will make jumping out of your comfort zone less scary.

MONEY MAGNET RITUAL

———

TIME FRAME: *40 days*

The Money Magnet Ritual helps you develop this prosperous and balanced mind-set. As you look at the Money Magnet Grid Sheet (page 94), write your intentions, place the crystals on the grid, and become clearer about your financial values. This ritual will help you magnetically attract the energy of money, abundance, and opportunity.

WHAT YOU'LL NEED:

———

8 Citrine stones for prosperity, light, and positivity

4 Tourmalinated Quartz stones to clear and unlock energy blockages

1 Peacock Ore stone for happiness and to transform negative energy into positive

1 Goldstone for confidence, abundance, and motivation

1 Kambaba Jasper stone for self-worth, courage, and personal growth

1 Clear Quartz stone for clarity, manifestation, and creation

1 Jade stone for wisdom, harmony, and wealth

2 Tiger's Eye stones for luck, good fortune, and good decisions

1 Pyrite stone for inner reflection, protection, and representation of the energy of gold

1 Carnelian stone for abundance, moving forward on a new path, creativity, and protection

1 Malachite stone for transformation and emotional balance

1 Aventurine stone for manifestation, abundance, and inner balance

1 Green Calcite stone for stability, healing, and success

2 small Clear Quartz points: 1 to activate your crystal grid and 1 for the center point of your grid

1 green candle

1 mala necklace

1 copy of the Money Magnet Grid Sheet (page 94)

1 blue pen—blue is the color of truth. It's believed that you're more likely to retain information when you write it with blue ink.

1 sage stick

1 feather

1 abalone shell or fireproof container to catch ashes from the sage

RITUAL STEPS:

This ritual should be started on a New Moon, symbolic of new beginnings,
or within a 3-day period before or after the New Moon.
Consult a Moon phase calendar for the most current information.

———

1. Sage your environment, and cleanse your crystals (page 22).

2. Place all the crystals in one area. Sitting in front of them, close your eyes and take 3 deep breaths. Aloud or in your head, say the following: *"I ask that the highest vibration of love and light connect with my highest self to clear all unwanted energy and any previous programming. I command these crystals to hold the intention of prosperity, new opportunities, and abundance in all areas of my life. Thank you, thank you, thank you."*

3. Find a place for your Money Magnet Grid where it will be undisturbed for 40 consecutive days.

4. Light the green candle next to your grid.

5. Write your Wealth Attraction Plan on your Money Magnet Grid. Look at each point on the grid, and think about each of these areas individually. The 8 points on the grid are symbolic of the 8 forms of wealth. In the blank space in the center of the grid, use the blue pen to write what you would like to manifest in your life. Be sure to write in the present tense. Then sign and date it as you would a contract. This is the most important contract of all because it's a contract with yourself. Then say, "Thank you, thank you, thank you," out loud.

6. Start placing the crystals individually on the Money Magnet Grid from the outside in as follows:

    a. Place one Citrine at each of the 4 corners of your Money Magnet Grid Sheet.

    b. Place the fifth Citrine above the words Wealth Goals.

    c. Place the Kambaba Jasper above the words Invest in You.

    d. Place the Jade on top of the words Be Generous.

    e. Place the Malachite below the words Take Action.

    f. Place the sixth Citrine below the words Have Faith.

    g. Place the Green Calcite below the words Healthy Mind, Body, & Spirit.

    h. Place the Clear Quartz on top of the words Clear Intention.

    i. Place the Peacock Ore above the words Positive Attitude.

    j. Place a Tourmalinated Quartz in the Wealth Goals, Be Generous, Have Faith, and Clear Intention triangles.

k. Place the Pyrite in the Invest in You triangle.

l. Place the Carnelian in the Take Action triangle.

m. Place the Aventurine in the Healthy Mind, Body, & Spirit triangle.

n. Place the Goldstone in the Positive Attitude triangle.

o. Place the 2 Tiger's Eye stones below the Pyrite and above the Aventurine within the Wealth Attraction Plan box.

p. Place the 2 remaining Citrine stones above the Carnelian and below the Goldstone within the Wealth Attraction Plan box. (For more guidance, see the photo on page 90.)

q. Place 1 Clear Quartz point in the center of your grid.

7. Starting from the outside with a Citrine stone, take the second Clear Quartz point, and draw an invisible line between the stones to energetically connect each to the next. Think of it as "connecting the dots" like when you were a kid.

8. This step is a very important part of the ritual—it's the "secret sauce": Chant the mantra below aloud 108 times on a set of mala beads, using each bead to keep count. Do this every day for 40 days. For optimum results, the mantra should be chanted at the same time each day. If you miss a day, you must start the whole ritual over at day 1 again. This part of the ritual is essential, as it helps to reprogram your brain. Mantras have been used by yogis and mystics for thousands of years. Every time you chant a mantra, you tap out a particular sequence, rhythm, and position that initiates a chemical reaction in the brain and body. It's as if you have an electronic security system in your mouth. Punch in the right code on the upper palate, and you gain entry to the brain and your inner chambers of higher consciousness.

Ganesha Mantra: *This mantra is believed to give you material and spiritual prosperity. Lord Ganesha is the Hindu elephant-headed deity who is widely revered as the remover of obstacles, often bestowing success on new ventures and bringing financial abundance. Below is one of Lord Ganesha's mantras, which has been used for centuries:*

Om Gum Ganapatayei Namaha (Pronunciation: Aum Gum Gah-nah-pah-tah-yay Nah-mah-ha) It's believed that this mantra should be recited before starting a new business venture to bring success, good luck, wealth, and peace. It assists in warding off negativity in your life.

9. When you're finished chanting your mantra, end your ritual by putting out the candle.

10. Each day for 40 days, repeat steps 8 and 9.

Money Magnet Grid

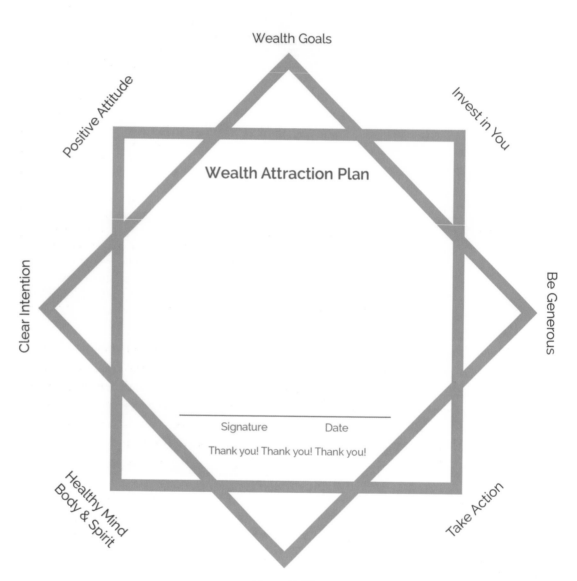

Wealth Goals

Positive Attitude

Invest in You

Wealth Attraction Plan

Clear Intention

Be Generous

Healthy Mind
Body & Spirit

Take Action

Have Faith

Signature   Date

Thank you! Thank you! Thank you!

Citrine

THE LIGHT MAKER

COLOR: Light yellow or golden yellow

ORIGIN: Found in many places, including Brazil, Madagascar, and the U.S.

HISTORY AND LORE: Derived from the French word *citron*, meaning lemon, this crystal's vibe is anything but sour! Sweet is the essence of this fortune-flourishing gem. Used in the jewelry of Greek and Roman civilizations dating back to the 1st century A.D., citrine has long been remarked upon for its subtle, honeyed beauty. Citrine is known as the money stone because it is believed to elevate optimism and energy, and therefore bring you to a place of opportunity, prosperity, and abundance.

HEALING PROPERTIES: The sunny attitude of Citrine cultivates an energy that is fertile for growth. In working with the solar plexus chakra, it warms the core to radiate power, centeredness, confidence, and endurance. Citrine is unique because it is one of few stones that rather than absorbing negative energy, clears it. It makes room for happiness and light, allowing the spirit to welcome a wide range of positive possibilities. Think of Citrine as the friend you call when you need a pick-me-up, the one who never fails to brighten your day. This upbeat crystal will be your cheerleader, rooting you on when you need a win.

BELIEVE IN WHAT'S POSSIBLE FOR YOU!

Some stories are so incredible that no one would believe you didn't make them up. Years ago, a man from out of the area called us wanting to purchase a Prosperity Necklace, but he didn't have a bank account or credit card. He told us that he believed in miracles and that once he saved enough money, he would send us a money order for the necklace. Every now and then, he would call and check in, letting us know that he was still saving his money. We loved talking to him; he was always upbeat and positive.

Months went by, but sure enough, one day we received his money order for the Prosperity Necklace. I often wonder who was more excited about it, him or us. A man we had only met over the phone had given us such a blessing. He taught us to never give up, to have a positive attitude regardless of our circumstances, and to believe in miracles.

The following month, he called. "You're never going to believe what happened! I've been wearing the Prosperity Necklace, and I won the lotto—well over a million dollars!" We all screamed together on the phone; it was a surreal moment. To this day, it's one of the best prosperity stories we've ever been blessed enough to be a part of.

LUCKY 7s RITUAL

TIME FRAME: *As long as you'd like!*

This is a fun, quick, and easy method to attract money your way! Not only will you attract money for yourself, but you'll pay it forward and help others become money magnets as well.

WHAT YOU'LL NEED:

8 "number 7" $1 bills. This means that all the bills must have the number 7 as their Federal Reserve District number (see the photo on page 97).

1 small Clear Quartz point

1 Pyrite stone

1 Aventurine stone

RITUAL STEPS:

1. Start by looking in your wallet for $1 bills with 7 as their Federal Reserve District number. The whole point is to collect the bills organically. If you buy something and use cash, be on the lookout for any bills with the number 7 among your change. Have fun with this process; there's no time limit.

2. Part of the secret to attracting money is sharing it with others. Once you have collected your 8 bills, give one of them away to someone so that they can start their own "game."

3. Now, you're left with 7 number 7 $1 bills. It's important to keep them together at all times. Place them in an area where they'll be undisturbed, with the crystals on top of them to enhance their energy. Let the money flow!

"Money is such an amazing teacher: What you choose to do with your money shows whether you are truly powerful or powerless."

— SUZE ORMAN,
author and financial advisor

CHAPTER 7

BREAKDOWN TO BREAKTHROUGH

TURNING THE DARKEST OF LIFE'S TRIALS INTO OPPORTUNITIES FOR GROWTH

"Rock bottom became the solid foundation on which I rebuilt my life."

— J.K ROWLING,
novelist and screenwriter

IN OUR FIFTH YEAR OF RUNNING ENERGY MUSE, WE OFFICIALLY ENTERED WHAT I CALL THE "BUSINESS SCHOOL OF HARD KNOCKS." THERE'S no way to sugarcoat it, so I'll just say it: We were drowning in financial debt. In the world of energy, this is called a major first chakra issue. In the business world, the terminology is more blatant: "You're screwed."

We had been invited to participate in a high-end retail spa show. This was exactly the venue we needed to expand our company into a larger marketplace. The only problem was that the show was in Cancún, Mexico, and would be expensive to attend. But what we were doing at the time wasn't working. It was time to switch things up and try something new, so despite the financial risk, we decided to roll the dice and place a bet on Cancún.

Our mild-mannered, business-savvy accountant—let's call him Kyle—was in shock when we told him of our plans to spend money on a trip when we were already in debt. He had warned us about becoming financially overextended with our overstaffing, heavy inventory, and "unconventional" expenses.

I could tell he had had enough of us by the tone of his voice and the look on his face. "Can you please explain the ridiculous expenditures at a store called Get Lucky Bamboo? Or why you hired a shaman to bless your business? And this is the best one yet—a 500-pound Amethyst crystal."

I cleared my throat and said with full authority, "I know these charges seem extraneous, but we work with energy. To shift energy, we need out-of-the-box techniques. Come on, you know we're not your standard corporate America clients."

"Obviously! I've known that since the day I met you two," he responded.

"Since you asked about the shaman," I continued, "here's why we felt it was necessary: We realized we never had our business officially blessed to bring in positivity, blessings, and financial abundance. And the Amethyst crystal had an unexplainable energy about it. The moment we saw it, we knew it had come into our lives for a reason: to help us with our business. We need it to hold the vibration of abundance until Timmi and I can work through our current poverty consciousness issues. We added the bamboo for good Feng Shui. Our east quadrant in the showroom was completely devoid of life. Now, it's flourishing with living bamboo, which represents upward mobility. It's all coming together for us, Kyle!"

Timmi was more pragmatic. "We know you're confused about our decision to go to Cancún. The financial timing isn't good, but we feel it's important that we go there to introduce Energy Muse to a new market."

Kyle was silent.

I jumped in again. "Did you know that money is just an exchange of energy? We're in debt because our personal energy is blocked. We're not in the flow, so our money isn't flowing either."

More silence.

I pressed on. "To shift our financial energy, we must be reinspired, see life through a new set of eyes, and move beyond the finances. It's important for us to tap into our gifts so that we can share those gifts with our customers and help them. Right now, we're so consumed with fear that we've lost sight of our goal of educating people on the healing properties of crystals. On this trip, we'll have the opportunity to start over again. In the Riviera Maya, there's a pre-Hispanic spiritual purification ceremony similar to a sweat lodge called a *Temazcal*. It purifies your body, mind, and spirit, and gives you the feeling of being rebirthed or reborn!"

Timmi nodded and added, "Maybe after the Temazcal, our finances will be reborn, and we can have a fresh start."

We sat back and waited. Finally, after a very uncomfortable silence, Kyle cleared his throat, straightened his tie, and put his pen on the table. Then, in an uncharacteristically loud voice, he shouted, "Are you both insane?!"

This wasn't the first time we'd heard this. Our family and friends often questioned our business logic. When I told my mom of our upcoming trip, she said, "Smart people don't go on trips and spend more money when they're already in debt. I know no one is going to stop you from doing what you want to do, but I'm curious—will you be celebrating Mother's Day with me this year since it's on the Sunday of the week you're gone?"

Timmi's mom shared a similar opinion. "Isn't it possible to create more business in the U.S. instead of traveling to Mexico?" Timmi was also expected to attend the family Mother's Day dinner that her mom was hosting.

They all had a point. The responsible choice—from a financial and familial perspective—would be to skip Cancún, but our minds were made up. We were going, and that was that.

How did it turn out? Unfortunately, the spa show was a complete bust. Our luck hit an all-time low. People loved the energy and beauty of the crystals, but there was one major concern—importing fees. Everyone felt this additional cost would price the crystals and jewelry out of the market. Our gamble hadn't paid off, and we were now in even more of a financial hole.

While packing our booth up for the day, a woman named Bertha walked over and introduced herself. She told us that she was a healer who had grown up in a family of healers in Cancún and was very interested in learning more about crystals. The minute I heard this, I asked if she knew anyone who could lead a Temazcal for us. She grinned from ear to ear. "Yes, my good friend is a very respected shaman. Would you like me to call him for you?"

The stars had suddenly aligned for us! Bertha agreed to be our tour guide. She showed us sacred sites and coordinated a Temazcal with her friend. In exchange, we shared more information with her about crystals.

The day before our two-hour purification ceremony, the Temazcal, we visited the Mayan ruins. It seemed fitting, as our financial life was also in ruins!

The next day, we visited the ancient pyramid El Castillo. There, we planted Quartz crystals in the ground near the pyramid steps to seed our intentions of light, gratitude, and peace on Earth. We made a wish in the magical waters of El Paraiso. It's said that if you dive underwater there and make a wish, it will come true. Timmi and I both knew what we wanted to wish for. Without saying a word, we dove deep into the ocean and wished for a financial miracle.

At dusk, we drove down a long, secluded road, deep into the jungle. When the trees parted, a breathtaking ecological reserve appeared. We followed a Mayan shaman named Gabriel down a candlelit pathway past a house with images of Mayan gods etched on the walls. The energy buzzed at a high frequency. We felt as if we had been transported back in time.

When we reached the end of the path, we saw a round, igloo-shaped Temazcal—the womb of Mother Earth. Before we entered it, Gabriel purified us with copal smoke and chanted softly. We crawled into the womb on our knees through a small, south-facing opening.

Once we were inside, it was hot and dark. The ceremony lasted for well over 90 minutes. We prayed, let go, and purified ourselves. Childhood wounds reemerged, as outdated beliefs and negative thoughts melted away. In that moment, we had no debt, fear, or desperation about how we were going to make money. It was all just an illusion, created in our minds.

In the darkness, we realized that we are spirit. We are light. We are energy. We aren't contained in this human vessel. We're so much more! Our souls have an everlasting resonance. This out-of-body experience made us feel connected to the Earth and the cosmos at the same time. In that moment, we knew the truth, and we were purified of our self-imposed illusions. We were set free.

When the ceremony ended, we crawled out of the Temazcal and were greeted by the sparkling stars in the sky. In the middle of the jungle, in an adobe dome, we experienced the wisdom of facing fear and looking inward. We connected with the wisdom of endurance, courage, purification, and healing. We ended the night by swimming in a cenote, a sacred well or sinkhole that some believe the Mayans used as a portal to speak with the gods. It was a powerful day of spiritual awakening that would shift our lives forever.

The next day, on the way to the airport, we were faced with the reality of our dire financial situation. Not only were we going home further in debt, but we knew we'd be hearing "I told you so" from everyone who had advised us not to go. What were we going to do to get out of this mess?

GOING HOME WITH OUR TAILS BETWEEN OUR LEGS

Due to the combination of our financial problems and the intense spiritual work of the Temazcal, I felt like I was on the verge of a mental breakdown. I became violently ill and told myself it was just Montezuma's revenge. I had cold sweats and spent a lot of time in the bathroom. I practically crawled onto the airplane. Then I couldn't control my tears. All my emotions flooded to the surface, and there was nowhere to hide during the flight home.

Timmi, on the other hand, felt great. She had purged her past and released her fears, leaving her with that "top of the world" feeling. She frequently turned to me on the plane, teasing me about being a baby and telling me I needed to get over it.

When I arrived home, my family was waiting for me to celebrate Mother's Day. I quickly hugged my mom, immediately ran to the bathroom, and then went to bed. Not only did I feel physically horrible, I also felt guilty because I couldn't celebrate Mother's Day with my mom and kids. Obviously, I wasn't winning any Mother (or Daughter) of the Year awards.

Timmi headed over to her mom's house for the family Mother's Day dinner. Unlike me, who was having an intense physical reaction to the purging of emotions, Timmi was holding everything together . . . or so she thought.

She walked into the house, feeling better than she had felt in years. "Hey, everyone! Happy Mother's Day!" she said. As they sat down at the dinner table, Timmi asked her husband, Jim, if he had remembered to pick up the gift for her grandma. When he apologized for forgetting, in the blink of an eye, Timmi transformed from Gandhi to a self-righteous brat.

In front of everyone, she rolled her eyes and remarked, "Of course you did. I should have known this would happen. I should have just taken care of it myself. Then it would have been done right."

Timmi's mom, Terry, looked at her in complete shock and horror. "Well, Jim was taking care of your kids while you were off being 'spiritually enlightened' in Mexico. Maybe you should give him a break."

As dinner progressed, the emotions built. Every little thing bugged Timmi, from the clinking of the forks to the way people breathed, to the "non-spiritual" conversations around the table. Her head started pounding. *Why am I here? I feel terrible*, she thought.

Then the gift exchange began. At a breaking point, Timmi turned to her mom and said, "I have the perfect gift for you. This book has helped me to become compassionate, loving, and gracious. I think you would really benefit from this."

Terry looked Timmi in the eyes and said, "You should really follow through with the things you read."

Timmi's jaw hit the ground. "Excuse me?!" Her mom repeated herself. The whole room went silent.

"I do!" Timmi screamed. "I'm on a spiritual path!" She proceeded to flip off her mother and exclaimed, "Fuck off!" in front of everyone. Then she stormed out, leaving her mom and family in disbelief on Mother's Day. Yes, the Temazcal purge had finally hit her and hit her hard.

Seventeen hours later, after some much-needed rest, Timmi awoke horrified by her uncharacteristic episode the night before. She called me and confessed what had happened with her mom. She felt physically ill from the guilt. I couldn't believe Timmi had acted that way—it was so unlike her. I suggested she get off the phone and send her mom the biggest, most beautiful bouquet of flowers with a simple note that read, "I'm sorry. I love you, Mom."

THE CHALLENGES OF A SPIRITUAL PATH

Being on a spiritual path is not all unicorns and rainbows. It stops you in your tracks and kicks you in the ass when you least expect it. You have ups, but then you have downs. You aren't blissed out all the time. Why? Because as you become clearer, you see the truth. This clarity doesn't always make life easier. It forces you to

be honest with yourself and take ownership of what you've created. It's as if every step forward takes you into the unknown, and when you turn around to walk back into the safety of your comfort zone, there's no longer a door to get back in. You're forced to move forward, knowing the old way no longer exists.

After our intense break*down* came our break*through*. We realized that we already held within us all the necessary tools to be spiritually and financially successful. Instead of relying on others to solve our problems, we had to take responsibility and solve them ourselves. By shifting our perspective, we were able to see our financial debt as an opportunity to grow, rather than viewing it as a burden. This awareness changed our business from that day forward, and a huge breakthrough did happen, clearing the path for a new beginning: David Beckham was spotted in public wearing our jewelry only days after we returned. The image went viral, catapulting our business to new levels.

Maybe there *was* some wisdom to the shaman's blessing, strategically placing the bamboo, having the Amethyst hold the space for abundance, and purging our fears?

Trust us, there was!

HITTING ROCK BOTTOM

One of the biggest lessons we learned from our trip is that when you stir up energy with deep healing work, it's vital that you give yourself enough time to process it. You may need to temporarily retreat in order to come back into balance. Obviously, Timmi and I were not ourselves when we returned. We missed that very important step of getting grounded before reentering our everyday lives.

On the spiritual path, it's easy to become enchanted by new ideas and heart-opening ways to tap into the "real you." But as the real you emerges, remember that not everyone around you is going through the same transformation.

This doesn't mean that you need to avoid or leave people who aren't in your new frequency. It simply means you need to be patient with yourself and know that you're in a time of change and healing. As you become more connected to your truth, you'll know which mind and heart space you're in. You will also know if it's time to take action or to retreat.

Smoky Quartz

WISDOM KEEPER:
LEAVE YOUR BAGGAGE BEHIND

COLOR: Light to dark smoky gray and brown

ORIGIN: Found in many locations, including Australia, Brazil, Madagascar, Scotland, and the U.S.

HISTORY AND LORE: When Smoky Quartz enters a room, it (metaphorically) opens all the windows and lets in all the light. It clears the dust. With its deep brown tint, Smoky Quartz has been used in mourning jewelry since the 16th century, and was especially popular in Victorian-era Britain.

HEALING PROPERTIES: If something no longer serves you, Smoky Quartz gives you the clarity to let it go. Working with Smoky Quartz helps you to overcome negative emotions like stress, fear, anger, jealousy, and even feelings of depression. It's often referred to as a "mood elevator" stone. Smoky Quartz is a gemstone that connects you to the energies of the Earth, helping you to keep both feet on the ground and remain balanced in any situation. It's an ideal crystal to be used in grounding, centering, and stabilizing energies, but it also aids in removing negative energy from your body. It's a wonderful tool for clearing the mind during any meditation practice and is one of the best crystals to use with the root chakra.

GROUNDED TO THE CORE RITUAL

A spiritual awakening isn't a quick fix. It isn't something anyone else can do for you or that you can wrap up in a few days. The process can take years. It isn't about the final destination because, in reality, there is no final destination. As the saying goes, "It's about the journey," and what you learn about yourself along the way. This ritual will help you become balanced and grounded back into the Earth when everything else in your life feels as if it's spinning out of control.

WHAT YOU'LL NEED:

2 Hematite spheres that fit into the palms of your hands for grounding, balance, and focus

1 Smoky Quartz crystal for centering and stabilizing energies

1 sage stick

1 feather

1 abalone shell or fireproof container to catch ashes from the sage

RITUAL STEPS:

Ideally, this ritual should be done outside with bare feet on the Earth. If this isn't an option, you can do it indoors. The most important thing is that you do it! This is definitely a simple ritual that can be done daily.

1. Sage your environment, and cleanse your crystals (page 22).
2. Hold the crystals in your hands, close your eyes, and take 3 deep breaths. Aloud or in your head, say the following: *"I ask that the highest vibration of love and light connect with my highest self to clear all unwanted energy and any previous programming. I command these crystals to hold the intention of becoming balanced, grounded, and aligned with the Earth's energy. Thank you, thank you, thank you."*
3. Stand with your feet slightly parted and firmly planted on the ground. (If it's more comfortable, you can sit in a chair with your feet firmly on the ground.)
4. Place the Smoky Quartz between your feet, and hold the Hematite spheres in your hands.

5. Take 3 deep breaths in through the nose and out through the mouth.
6. With each exhalation, move your awareness to your first chakra (located at your tailbone). Silently say, *I am grounding my energy into the core of the Earth.*
7. Visualize a white ball of light spinning within your body between your hips. See this light expanding, filling your first chakra. Visualize this light traveling from your hips down to your knees and to your feet.
8. Visualize a thick cord—a few inches in diameter—filled with light and growing from the sole of each foot, traveling down to the core of the Earth. See the cords from your feet become one as they dive deeper and deeper into the crystal core of the Earth.
9. See the cords rooting into this crystal core, and allow yourself to feel centered and connected. Release all your fears, burdens, anger, and unresolved issues into the light, propelling them down the cord into the Earth.
10. Inhale deeply. Starting at the core of the Earth, see the intertwined cord fill with white light. Visualize the light traveling back up the cord, separating into two balls of light as the cord splits into two and enters the soles of your feet.
11. Visualize the two balls moving up to your knees and rejoining at your first chakra.
12. As you finish your visualization, gently open your eyes. You are now grounded.

Chrysocolla

IT'S ALL ABOUT NEW BEGINNINGS

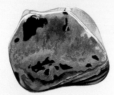

COLOR: Blue green

ORIGIN: Found in many locations, including Australia, England, Israel, Mexico, the U.S., and the Democratic Republic of the Congo

HISTORY AND LORE: Chrysocolla was the original chill pill. This crystal has been helping people embrace their "inner mellow" since the time of Cleopatra. Named by the ancient Greek philosopher Theophrastus, Chrysocolla translates to "gold glue." It was often used by ancient Egyptians in jewelry soldering to bond with gold, hence its name. Cleopatra was said to wear Chrysocolla everywhere because of its calming, feminine power.

HEALING PROPERTIES: This crystal connects to the heart and throat chakras to promote balanced, thoughtful communication and tranquility. If you need to seriously destress, calm your nerves with the soothing blue energy of Chrysocolla. It works well to eliminate tensions in the home, or in an end-of-the-day purifying bath.

CRYSTAL MEDICINE WHEEL RITUAL

TIME FRAME: *40 days*

From Stonehenge to the Egyptian pyramids, many sacred stone structures have been built throughout history. Native Americans constructed sacred medicine wheels, laying stones on the Earth in a specific arrangement. Medicine wheels are used in rituals for healing, introspection, celebration, enlightenment, meditation, and prayer. They're believed to create movement and change.

This ritual will teach you how to construct your own crystal medicine wheel, which will act as an overview of the ebb and flow of life. The act of placing each crystal in your wheel is symbolic of the phases, cycles, and lessons we all have in life. This medicine wheel will take you through the cycles of life, where you have to break down to break through so that you can grow and begin again. Then the cycle starts over, playing out differently every time. Each crystal will reveal a unique message for you as you travel around the wheel.

As each of us becomes more aware of this cycle of life and we start to heal ourselves, we realize how vital it is to heal the energy of the Earth. We are one with the Earth.

WHAT YOU'LL NEED:

A space that's at least 20" x 20"

A pinch of tobacco as an offering to the Great Spirit

Crystal Medicine Wheel Diagram (page 110)

Crystal Medicine Wheel Stone Placement and Meaning chart (page 111)

A blue pen—blue is the color of truth. It's believed that you're more likely to retain information when you write it in blue ink.

A journal

The 36 stones listed in the chart on page 111

1 Clear Quartz point to activate your crystal grid

1 sage stick

1 feather

1 abalone shell or fireproof container to catch ashes from the sage

Crystal Medicine Wheel Diagram

Crystal Medicine Wheel
Stone Placement and Meaning

POSITION	CRYSTAL	CRYSTAL MEANING	POSITION	CRYSTAL	CRYSTAL MEANING
1	Clear Quartz point or cluster	Clarity, gratitude, and connecting to the Divine	19	Carnelian	Bonding, ancestors, family, and relationships
2	Chrysocolla	Patience and self-reflection	20	Garnet	Passion and inner power
3	Citrine	Life purpose and yang energy	21	Amethyst	Rationality and practicality
4	Moonstone	Internal rhythms and yin energy	22	Bloodstone	Conquering your fears and shadow side
5	Petrified Wood	Grounding and stability	23	Malachite	Igniting change and versatility
6	Malachite	Purification and transformation	24	Obsidian	Perceiving and mirroring the feelings of others
7	Pyrite	Manifestation, vitality, and taking action	25	Shungite	Healing and detoxifying your mind, body, and spirit
8	Indigo Gabbro	Transformation, emergence, and rites of passage	26	Aventurine	Self-love, joy, and positivity
9	Tree Agate	Earth element—centered and rooted	27	Quartz	Purity and clarity
10	Selenite	Air element—higher consciousness and spiritual awakening	28	Sodalite	Spontaneity and openness
11	Ocean Jasper	Water element—fluidity and change	29	Jade	Abundance and wisdom
12	Mookaite	Fire Element—forgiveness and letting go	30	Labradorite	Truth and illumination
13	Clear Quartz	Clarity and amplification	31	Fluorite	Growth and healthy boundaries
14	Hematite	Rest and relaxation	32	Blue Lace Agate	Trust and expression
15	Blue Apatite	Healing and truth	33	Rose Quartz	Unconditional love and acceptance
16	Sunstone	Fearlessness and courage	34	Black Tourmaline	Focus and knowledge
17	Chrysocolla	Inner balance and perseverance	35	Dumortierite	Meditation, empowerment, and self-reflection
18	Moss Agate	Connection with nature and consistency	36	Tiger's Eye	Strength and endurance

RITUAL STEPS:

———

1. Sage your environment, and cleanse your crystals (page 22).

2. Place all your stones where you'll be constructing your medicine wheel and sit in front of them. Close your eyes, and take 3 deep breaths. Aloud or in your head, say the following: *"I ask that the highest vibration of love and light connect with my highest self to clear all unwanted energy and any previous programming. I command these crystals to hold the intention of healing, awareness, and love. Thank you, thank you, thank you."*

3. Go outside and make an offering to the Earth. An offering is an important way to give back to Mother Earth for all that she gives to us. Take the tobacco in one hand, and raise the offering to the sky while saying, "This is an offering to the sky. Thank you for the air that we breathe."

4. Touch the tobacco to the ground, and release it there, saying, "Thank you for providing us a home that we can live upon."

5. Now you're ready to create your medicine wheel in your space! Set up your medicine wheel in the area you have designated so that it won't be disturbed for 40 days. The purpose of this ritual is reflection, growth, and clarity—and these things take time.

6. Refer to the Crystal Medicine Wheel Diagram and Crystal Medicine Wheel Stone Placement and Meaning chart on pages 110 and 111 for guidance in placing your crystals while creating your medicine wheel. Don't rush the process. Take time to feel the energy of each stone as you place it in the appropriate space.

7. Once you've finished placing all the stones, activate your crystal grid with the Clear Quartz point. Starting from the outside with the Tree Agate, use the point to draw an invisible line between the stones to energetically connect them to one another. Think of it as "connecting the dots" like when you were a kid. After you finish, take a moment to gaze at your beautiful creation.

8. When you're ready, quietly sit in front of your medicine wheel with your eyes closed. Take 3 long, deep breaths in through the nose and out through the mouth.

9. On day 1, spend time focusing on stone 1, which is Quartz. It symbolizes clarity, gratitude, and connection to the divine. What do these words mean to you in your life right now? Think of what you can shift to invite more of these energies into your life.

10. After you've answered these questions in your head, write them down in your journal. Take some time to write out concrete ideas—a game plan—as to how you're going to make these changes happen.

11. Repeat steps 8 through 10 with a different stone every day until on day 36, you've made it all the way around your crystal medicine wheel.

12. On day 37, look at your notes from days 1 through 10. What did you write about these aspects? Do you need to add anything to your action plan? What wisdom did you extract from the experience?

13. On day 38, do the same with days 11 through 20.

14. On day 39, do the same with days 21 through 30.

15. On the last day—day 40—do the same with days 31 through 36.

16. Through this 40-day process, you're guaranteed to learn something about yourself! But you're not going to stop there. This process is ever evolving and ever changing. The cycle may stop, but you will begin anew.

Blue Lace Agate

WISDOM KEEPER:
TRUTH SERUM

COLOR: Sky blue with a white lacelike pattern

ORIGIN: Namibia

HISTORY AND LORE: It's said that if you're nervous during a speech, you should picture the audience naked. Or you could carry a piece of Blue Lace Agate. This is a new stone, just recently discovered. Unlike other forms of Agate that have been used since the time of the ancient Greeks, Blue Lace Agate was only discovered within the last 60 years. For such a newcomer, it has already established an impressive reputation for its metaphysical properties.

HEALING PROPERTIES: Blue Lace Agate connects to the throat chakra, empowering you to relax into your words. Instead of getting tripped up by unnecessary thoughts, this crystal will clear the blocks between mind and mouth. It allows you to express yourself in a way that is both authentic and articulate. Blue Lace Agate is the go-to touchstone for relieving anxiety and stress.

"Remind yourself that you cannot fail at being yourself."

— WAYNE DYER,
International best-selling author and inspirational speaker

CHAPTER 8

THE LOVE GURU

RITUALS TO ATTRACT LOVE, REKINDLE PASSION, LOVE YOURSELF, AND MEND THE HEART

"I don't stay single for long. I carry a lot of rose quartz, which attracts the male. Maybe I need to calm it down with the amethyst."

— KATY PERRY,
singer and songwriter

"WHY DO YOU HAVE A HUGE PYRAMID IN YOUR LIVING ROOM?" MY NOW-HUSBAND, JASON, BLURTED OUT when he entered my apartment for the first time.

"I . . . um . . . sleep under it," I mumbled, trying to read his reaction.

Jason and I had met on a blind date, and when I found out that he was from Springfield, Missouri, I thought I'd better wait awhile before inviting him to visit my apartment. Once he saw my space, he would be fully aware of what he was getting into with me.

After selling real estate, I had become a full-time Feng Shui consultant, and my specialty was love. My apartment was my own personal laboratory filled with hundreds of books, crystals, trickling water fountains, copper pyramids, aromatherapy oils, and endless other energetic gadgets. Little crystal grids, flower petal mandalas, and mini medicine wheels filled the floors.

Results seemed to come easier when I followed particular formulas, so my passion became figuring out what those formulas were. Each month, I would focus on a different interest, such as money, health, or mindfulness, and I'd move my crystals, grids, and sacred geometry accordingly.

One month, love was in the air, so I transformed my apartment into a modern-day love chamber that even the goddess Aphrodite would have been happy to call home. Everything was in its proper place. Pink and red peonies (the flower of love) sat in vases throughout the place, and a framed picture of a pair of cranes (symbols of longevity in relationships) hung on my wall. In the southwest part of my bedroom—the universal direction for love and relationship luck—I placed a pair of mandarin

Heather's first-ever Feng Shui reading

ducks, representing a happy relationship; two Rose Quartz hearts, holding the energy of love; and two red candles to bring in the energy of love.

At the time I was playing around with love energy, it was for my career and discovering how I could help other people with love. I wasn't looking to attract a new relationship. It just wasn't on my mind. Then, two weeks later, my life changed when I was set up with Jason.

After a few weeks of dating, I couldn't avoid showing him my apartment any longer. I knew it would be the ultimate test to see if our relationship could move forward or if we should just end it.

When he entered, he didn't say a word at first. I held my breath while his eyes darted back and forth. I waited for him to say something, *anything*.

After I told Jason about how I slept under the pyramid, he asked, "If you sleep under it, why isn't it in your bedroom?"

"Well, see, the energy is better in the living room, and since copper is an amplifier, I want it to amplify good energy."

That answer seemed to appease him for a moment. He stopped to think about what he'd just heard. Then he asked, "So, why exactly do you sleep under a copper pyramid?"

"It's actually really fascinating," I answered, trying to gauge his interest. "I heard it preserves whatever is under it. The Egyptians did their healing and rejuvenation rituals in the pyramids, and I was curious if I slept under it, if it would help me feel more rejuvenated and energized in the morning. I think it works."

Luckily, Jason didn't turn around and run out the door. I assumed he was having one of two thoughts: (1) *This girl is completely crazy but one of the most unique women I've ever met*, or (2) *Wait until the guys in Missouri hear about this!*

Instead he said, "That's pretty cool! Can I sit under it?" I had to smile. And that was just the beginning.

Jason and I got married within one year of the day we met. Ironically, even though I wasn't trying to attract love for myself, my love ritual worked for me anyway. That's how powerful it is! Not only was I able to attract a lasting partner for myself, but I've seen this ritual work countless times to bring more love into others' lives, too—whether that means self-love, attracting a new relationship, or finding a soul mate.

FENG SHUI LOVE KILLERS

While this isn't a Feng Shui book, we can't resist offering you a few tips, along with information about using crystals to attract love. So, here are a few Feng Shui love killers to avoid. They can stop the flow of love from entering your life. Not every sign applies to everyone. But in general, it's a good rule of thumb to pay attention to these basics if you're looking for love, regardless of your gender.

- Dead plants outside the front door are nonwelcoming. Remedy: Always throw out dead plants immediately.

- A bedroom filled with artwork showing only one person usually results in a single person alone at night in bed. Remedy: Artwork should contain two people who symbolize a loving partnership.

- Mirrors in the bedroom that make a second image of the bed create the potential for infidelity or a third party who interferes with the relationship. Sometimes the third party can be an intrusive in-law or family member. Remedy: Cover mirrors in bedrooms with a curtain or loose fabric.

- A bed flush against a wall that can only be entered from one side symbolizes not making room for someone to enter your life. Remedy: Move the bed to the center of the room where it can be entered from both sides.

- Sleeping under a beam that divides the bed vertically brings separation or a loss of connection in the relationship. Remedy: Cover the beam with a curtain.

- Having black as your number-one clothing color choice in your closet closes down the energy of the heart chakra. Remedy: Don't wear black over your chest for 40 days. You can still wear black pants and jackets, but no black over the chest! Wearing colors such as pink, green, coral, rose, white, and blue will shift your energy immediately.

ATTRACT LOVE RITUAL

TIME FRAME:
40-day ritual + 3 days of prep

This is a 40-day ritual that should start on a New Moon. The preparation for this ritual will begin 3 days before it starts. Each day of prep consists of tasks that ready the mind, body, spirit, and space for the journey on which you are about to embark. It really works, so if you're ready to have a love breakthrough, fully dedicate yourself to every moment of this ritual!

Our friend Sally Lyndley, a successful fashion stylist in Los Angeles, was looking for love. I quickly learned she had almost all the Feng Shui killers working against her—she wore only black, her bed was against the wall, photographs of single women lined her space, and her office desk was in the corner of her bedroom so that the first thing she saw in the morning was work.

Sally was ready, so she fully committed to the Attract Love Ritual. She immediately used her stylist talents, shifting her wardrobe from all black to all pink, to tell the universe she was open to love.

The ritual tested her on the 15th day, when it brought an old boyfriend back into her life to see if she was still interested. She wasn't. On the 24th day, her typical romantic type—the "bad boy"—showed up, tempting her into a relationship that would go nowhere. She passed the test and continued with her ritual.

Here's what Sally has to say about her experience: "On the 36th day of my love ritual, I met my now-boyfriend, whom I now consider my life partner—not to mention, I gained so many great friends in the days before that, too! The issues that had caused problems in my past relationships are not occurring in this new partnership because of our open communication, love, and respect for each other."

Sally also found that the ritual increased her self-love a great deal. "When it was finished, I had a far more compassionate and loving relationship with myself than I had ever been able to truly create before."

Are you ready to try it for yourself?

PREPARATION

3 Days until the New Moon: Bedroom Prep

Getting ready for this powerful ritual requires some work. The first place to start is in the bedroom. Modifying the space to include a greater sense of Feng Shui will open it up to receive the energy of love.

WHAT YOU'LL NEED:

A plastic tub

5 lemons

1 cup distilled vinegar

1 sage stick

1 feather

1 abalone shell or fireproof container to catch ashes from the sage

Palo Santo incense

BEDROOM PREP STEPS:

1. Remove any pictures or gifts that you received from past partners. These items can be given away or stored in a box for the duration of the ritual. Put the box in a garage, an attic, or a closet that isn't in your bedroom.

2. Enhance love Feng Shui by removing all mirrors in the bedroom. If it isn't possible to remove the mirrors, you can cover them with a sheet or curtain. Place a sheet over the TV in the bedroom while not in use, or better yet, move the TV to a different room. Remove all images or landscape art that only contain single people. While you're at it, remove all pictures of family and friends from the bedroom.

3. Clean your bedroom. Declutter, throw away old magazines, dust, vacuum, change your sheets, and wash all the windows.

4. Energetically cleanse the room. Fill a plastic tub with water. Squeeze the juice of 5 lemons in the water, and add 1 cup of distilled vinegar. Using a clean cloth, wipe the doorknobs, as well as the front and back of all doors in your home.

5. To rid the space of negative energy, burn sage starting at the front door and walking counterclockwise around each room in your home. Ask the spirit of the sage to release any stuck, stagnant, or unwanted energy. Open windows to allow smoke to exit your space. (See page 23 for information about using sage.)

6. Light the Palo Santo incense. Start at the front door and walk clockwise around each room, filling the space with positive energy and asking the spirit of the Palo Santo to bless your space and bring miracles into your life. (See page 25 for information about using Palo Santo.)

PREPARATION
2 Days until the New Moon: Purifying Bath

After your entire space has been cleansed, it's time to purify yourself with this bath.

WHAT YOU'LL NEED:

---

1 small box baking soda to strip your energy body of unwanted energies

1 cup sea salt to absorb any negative energy from your energy body

2 instant coffee bags (single serving) to cleanse your energy body

2 cups organic apple cider vinegar to purify your energy body

1 white candle—a symbolic way of letting spirit know you're connecting

1 sage stick

1 feather

1 abalone shell or fireproof container to catch ashes from the sage

PURIFYING BATH STEPS:

---

1. Sage your bathroom before bathing (page 23).
2. Fill the bathtub with warm water and the baking soda, sea salt, instant coffee bags, and organic apple cider vinegar.
3. Use your hands to mix the ingredients in the water as you say out loud, "I program this water to purify my mind, body, and soul."
4. Light the white candle, and place it in a safe place in the bathroom.
5. Bathe for 11 to 21 minutes.
6. While in the bath, visualize any situations that have caused you sadness, hurt, or pain in past relationships. Dip your head and body under the bath water at least 9 times—the number 9 symbolizes the ending of a cycle. This acts as a personal baptism. Imagine that you are free from the past.
7. Let the water drain as you continue to sit in the tub. Visualize all your hurts and pains draining away, no longer holding any space in your life. (Throw away the coffee bags in a trash can.)
8. When you've completed your bath, sage your bathroom again to purify anything that has been energetically released.

PREPARATION

1 Day until the New Moon: The Love Altar

On the day before the New Moon, create a love altar—a table that
represents your focused intention on attracting love. This space will help
to support your desires and allow you to cultivate a deeper love and understanding of yourself. The altar can be as simple or as elaborate as you
want to make it—the choice is yours. Just make sure your altar is always
clean and dust-free.

WHAT YOU'LL NEED:

A small table (altar)

A white lace or white tablecloth

1 Rose Quartz mala necklace or a Malachite mala necklace—whichever you feel more attracted to

2 pink candles to represent the energy of 2 people in a relationship

1 feather (any kind of feather that you feel spiritually connected to)

1 small bowl of water

1 pink crystal (Rose Quartz, Rhodonite, or Rhodochrosite) to hold the intention of receiving love

1 green crystal (Aventurine, Malachite, or Jade) to hold the intention of giving love

Stationery or a journal

1 blue pen—blue is the color of truth. It's believed that you're more likely to retain information when you write it with blue ink.

An image or statue symbolic of love like Aphrodite or Eros, a piece of jewelry that symbolizes love, or a picture of lovebirds

Love Altar Steps:

1. Add any other items that represent love to you, such as incense or flowers, and simply set up your altar in whatever way feels right to you.

2. Before you set up your altar, make sure you program your crystals. Hold them in your hands, close your eyes, and take 3 deep breaths. Aloud or in your head, say the following: *"I ask that the highest vibration of love and light connect with my highest self to clear all unwanted energy and any previous programming. I command these crystals to hold the intention of love, self-love, and attraction. Thank you, thank you, thank you."*

The Morning of the New Moon Steps:

1. Write down all the qualities of your ideal partner. It's important to handwrite this on paper; don't type it on a computer or iPad! Take your time, and be specific. Include 5 nonnegotiable items—things you aren't willing to compromise on. Then list 10 or more things you desire in a new partner.

2. As you take the time to focus on what you really want and what is nonnegotiable, you become very clear on who you wish to attract. When you're finished, date it, sign your name, and write, "Thank you, thank you, thank you!"

3. Fold this paper in half and then in half again so that it makes a square, and place it under your mattress where you sleep.

40-DAY LOVE RITUAL

The 40-day time period is designed to bring any issues about love to the surface and starts on the New Moon. An old love might come back into your life—someone you haven't spoken to in years. Often, this happens due to unresolved issues that were never discussed, and this gives you an opportunity to have closure from a different perspective. Sometimes old childhood wounds, anger, or sadness come up. At the same time, a new sense of joy, hope, and happiness emerges.

So, how can 40 days change your love life? It's a commitment to the process and a commitment to falling back in love with yourself that changes your love energy. By the end of the 40 days, you'll have a love breakthrough. How this plays out is different for everyone, but the end result is always the same—you'll love yourself more, and as your vibration rises, so will the energy of others who are attracted to you. The 40 days will take you through a soulful journey.

RITUAL STEPS FOR 40 DAYS:

1. On the New Moon, day 1 of the ritual, sage your environment. Feel free to sage as needed during the other 39 days.
2. Sit in front of your love altar.
3. Light your candles and incense.
4. Pick up your mala beads, and chant aloud one of the following mantras (based on the gender you wish to attract) 108 times. (There are 108 beads on a mala necklace, and each bead is one verse of the chant. See the Glossary on page 267.) This must be done once a day with no more than 24 hours between chants. If you miss a day, you must start back on day 1. This part of the ritual is very important and must be done for 40 consecutive days. These mantras are chanted to invite the feminine or masculine into your life.

For attracting a man, chant: *Sat Patim Dehi Parameshwara*
(Pronunciation: Sat Pah-teem Day-hee Pah-rahm-esh-wah-rah)

For attracting a woman, chant: *Om Shrim Shriyei Namaha*
(Pronunciation: Om Shreem Shree-yay Nahm-ah-ha)

5. When you're finished chanting, place the mala beads back on your altar. Pick up the green and pink crystals, and hold them in your hands. Close your eyes, and set your intention by saying the following out loud: "I am love. I am lovable. I am worthy." Feel free to add anything else positive that you'd like to state about yourself.

6. Snuff out the candles when you're finished.

The Night of the New Moon: Take a Love Bath

WHAT YOU'LL NEED:

Rose or jasmine incense

1 red candle

1 pink candle

The petals from 12 fresh pink or red roses

1 bottle rose essential oil

1 bottle jasmine essential oil

Pink and green stones from your love altar

1 sage stick

1 feather

1 abalone shell or fireproof container to catch ashes from the sage

RITUAL STEPS FOR YOUR LOVE BATH:

1. Sage your bathroom (page 23).
2. Light and burn the rose or jasmine incense next to the tub.
3. Light two candles, one red and one pink, in the bathroom.
4. Add petals from 12 pink or red roses to the bathwater.
5. Add 6 drops of the rose oil and 6 drops of the jasmine oil to the bathwater.
6. Add the pink and green stones from your love altar to the bathwater.
7. During the bath, visualize yourself in a loving relationship, and place the stones over your heart.
8. Soak for 20 minutes.
9. Place the crystals back on the altar, and give the rose petals back to the Earth—place them on the grass or bury them in the soil. Don't throw them away in the trash!

FIRST COMES LOVE,
THEN COMES MARRIAGE

My wedding was featured on a TV show called *A Wedding Story*. The producers wanted to show how a ceremony could be both spiritual and religious by combining rituals from our Christian, Judaic, and Native American faiths. It became one of the show's most requested rerun episodes. I don't know if people wanted to emulate my wedding or if they were just fascinated by it.

What kinds of things did I do? My gift to my bridesmaids was a piece of Rose Quartz to represent my love and gratitude for each woman in my life. Then, as they walked down the aisle,

each of them held a crystal ball instead of a bouquet. The meaning behind the spherical shape is that it has no beginning and no end, representing everlasting love.

The wedding ceremony took place in the center of a medicine wheel, with each guest sitting in one of the four cardinal directions of north, south, east, or west. Peruvian drummers and flutists played ancient songs to honor our ancestors. Each guest was given bubbles to blow their wedding wishes and prayers into the sky after the ceremony. After our kiss, we were wrapped in an authentic Native American blanket. To this day, we sleep with that blanket on our bed every night.

Malachite

COLOR: Green

ORIGIN: Australia, Morocco, the U.S., and the Democratic Republic of Congo

HISTORY AND LORE: Malachite is a stone of wisdom. In ancient Egypt, Malachite lined the insides of pharaohs' headdresses because it was believed that the crystal would lend balance and insight to his rule. Dating as far back as 3000 B.C., Malachite, with its vibrant color, was ground into powder and used as eye makeup. Talk about having wise eyes!

HEALING PROPERTIES: Malachite is the ideal crystal for someone who has yet to find the right partner. Malachite can cleanse the chakras and help you see what is not working in your life. It's one of the most powerful transformational crystals for the heart. The emotional balance it provides will encourage you to take the action you need to remove negative patterns and enhance your transformational energy.

WISHES OF LOVE RITUAL:
A PRE-WEDDING CELEBRATION

TIME FRAME:
As long as it takes for all your loved ones to participate!

This Wishes of Love Ritual is one of the most meaningful rituals you can do with all your loved ones before the big day, such as at your wedding shower. It gives guests an opportunity to state out loud what they wish for you and your partner. We highly suggest this for any couple who wants to add another layer of love, happiness, and joy to their marriage. It's a powerful ritual that will continue to spread the love even after your wedding.

WHAT YOU'LL NEED:

1 bowl to hold the crystals

Enough Clear Quartz stones for each loved one participating to have a crystal

1 sage stick

1 feather

1 abalone shell or fireproof container to catch ashes from the sage

RITUAL STEPS:

1. Days before your celebration, cleanse and purify all the crystals (page 22). We suggest also letting them soak up the energy of the Sun for at least 1 hour and the energy of the Moon overnight.
2. If possible, sage the space where the event is being held.
3. When your guests arrive, give each person a Clear Quartz stone.
4. Ask your loved ones to gather in a circle, and place the bowl in the center.
5. Ask everyone to hold the stone in their hands and think of a wish or blessing they would like to make for the couple.
6. One by one, have each person state their wish out loud, then place the crystal into the bowl. This should continue until all crystals are in the bowl.
7. The crystals are now energized and programmed with wishes from all the people who mean the most to you. You can place this bowl in your bedroom, living room, or any special place in your home so that you can always feel the love.

SELF-LOVE

Timmi is a hopeless romantic, which is probably why she got married at 22. She always told me that she was going to live the American Dream—have a big house with a white picket fence with her golden retriever and four kids. She loved waking up early in the morning to create a custom loaf of bread with oatmeal, raisins, and dates using one of her favorite wedding gifts, the bread maker. After working out in the gym, she was off to her high-powered job in the garment industry and home by 6 P.M. to make dinner for her husband, Jim. She really was a happy homemaker in the morning, successful businesswoman by day, and doting wife at night. Life was good. She was indeed living the American Dream—what she had always wanted. For five years, she was in marital bliss . . . until the seven-year-itch came two years early.

The realization came one evening like a slap in the face. As she walked through the door and smelled the bread baking in the kitchen, something just didn't feel right. She poured two glasses of wine, sliced the bread, and she and her husband sat in silence as they ate dinner. They no longer had anything to say to each other, and it had been that way for more than a year. It was as if a wave of truth flooded Timmi's heart, and she understood that she'd been playing a role and living a lie. The American Dream that she

was brought up to believe in wasn't her dream at all. The man who sat in front of her was someone she didn't even know anymore. *Whose life am I living?* she wondered. She couldn't do it one day longer, so she left Jim.

This is when Timmi's dual Gemini personality emerged. I like to call her "evil Gemini twin Tammy." After Timmi left her marriage, she focused on her career and enjoyed living the life of a successful, financially independent woman. But by night, Tammy would come out . . . and she was wild. Life was to be lived fully, and that's what Tammy did. She drank excessively, worked out compulsively, shopped till she dropped, and even met a new man.

Suddenly she was in love, life was a party, and this was one party she hoped would never end. Timmi had everything she wanted, and she wanted even more of it. A year of extreme excess continued, but like all good parties, it did have to come to an end. One day while brushing her teeth, Timmi looked in the mirror and didn't recognize herself. Her parents barely spoke to her anymore, she was drinking and partying way too much, and it was starting to take its toll. A feeling of emptiness and loneliness filled her soul. Tammy, the evil twin, needed to go, and the real Timmi needed to reemerge. But just who was the real Timmi? This is when the road to healing and the way back home to herself began.

SELF-LOVE WHEEL RITUAL

TIME FRAME: *1 to 8 weeks*

Taking time to cultivate self-love is the greatest gift we can give ourselves, and it's the only way we can attract a loving relationship with someone else. This is the biggest lesson Timmi learned on her journey from playing a role to becoming her true self.

Choose to be the someone you would want to have in your life! By working with the Self-Love Wheel Ritual, you'll be on your way to finding the love you deserve.

Reach out to a friend or family member you trust, and share the ritual and your goals with that person. They will be your best cheerleader along the way and will keep you accountable and on track each week.

Some people use the excuse that there isn't enough time to stay committed to each week's intentions. You may need to give up something like binge watching your favorite TV show, trolling social media, or checking your e-mail every 5 minutes in order to make time for what's truly important—achieving the changes you desire in order to bring self-love into your life. After all, you are your best investment!

WHAT YOU'LL NEED:

A copy of the Self-Love Wheel (page 136)

1 Rose Quartz tumbled stone

1 Amazonite tumbled stone

1 Blue Apatite tumbled stone

1 Carnelian tumbled stone

1 Red Jasper tumbled stone

1 Moonstone tumbled stone

1 Clear Quartz tumbled stone

1 Bloodstone tumbled stone

1 blue pen—blue is the color of truth. It's believed that you're more likely to retain information when you write it with blue ink.

1 sage stick

1 feather

1 abalone shell or fireproof container to catch ashes from the sage

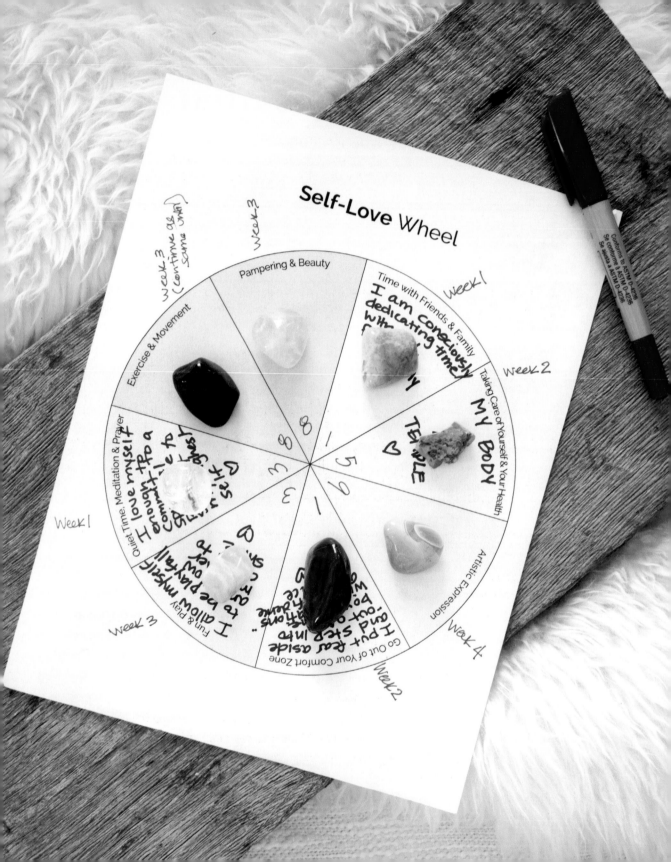

RITUAL STEPS:

1. Sage your environment, and cleanse your crystals (page 22).

2. Hold the crystals in your hands, close your eyes, and take 3 deep breaths. Aloud or in your head, say the following: *"I ask that the highest vibration of love and light connect with my highest self to clear all unwanted energy and any previous programming. I command these crystals to hold the intention of unconditional self-love, acceptance, and freedom from judgment. Thank you, thank you, thank you."*

3. Find a place where your Self-Love Wheel can remain undisturbed throughout the duration of the ritual.

4. The goal is to cultivate a more intimate relationship with yourself. Sit with your wheel in front of you. Each of the sections in the wheel represents an area to concentrate on in order to bring self-love into your life. Read each of the eight sections out loud.

5. How much time do you need to focus on each area of the Self-Love Wheel? You decide! Rate each area with a number between 1 and 10, with 1 as the least amount of time you need for that area and 10 as the most amount of time. Write your rating number in each specific area of your wheel.

6. Focus on any areas that have a ranking of 5 or higher. Write down one intention or action to take in order to see a change in that area. For example, if you wrote down 5 in the area of Exercise & Movement, your intention could be, "I commit to taking a 10-minute walk 3 times a week on Monday, Wednesday, and Sunday."

7. Now that you've finished writing down your intentions, gather your tumbled stones. The act of placing one tumbled stone in each of the areas of the wheel will ground the energy of your intention into reality. Place the stones accordingly:

   a. Rose Quartz in the Pampering & Beauty area
   b. Amazonite in the Time with Friends & Family area
   c. Blue Apatite in the Taking Care of Yourself & Your Health area
   d. Carnelian in the Artistic Expression area
   e. Red Jasper in the Go Out of Your Comfort Zone area
   f. Moonstone in the Fun & Play area
   g. Clear Quartz in the Quiet Time, Meditation, & Prayer area
   h. Bloodstone in the Exercise & Movement area

8. Decide which area you want to focus on first, and commit to your intention for 1 full week. It's best to start the ritual on Monday and end on Sunday.

9. This ritual could take 1 to 8 weeks. The timing depends on how many areas you choose to work on.

Self-Love Wheel

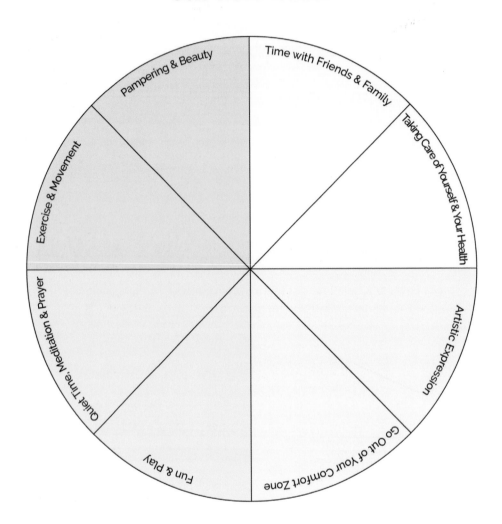

Rose Quartz

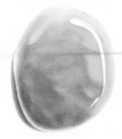

COLOR: Pink

ORIGIN: Found in many locations, including Brazil, India, Madagascar, and the U.S.

HISTORY AND LORE: Since the time of Greek myths, Rose Quartz has been thought to be the stone of unconditional love. Cupid, Roman god of desire and affection, was said to have bestowed Rose Quartz upon the Earth as a gift of love, passion, and happiness for all. Another legend tells a more tragic story. According to this myth, Ares, the Greek god of war, came in the form of a boar to kill Aphrodite's lover, Adonis. In trying to save Adonis, Aphrodite cut herself on a briar bush. As their blood spilled, it came together over a Quartz crystal, staining the stone pink. Zeus took pity on the lovers, and restored Adonis to Aphrodite for six months every year. It's because of this myth that Rose Quartz is thought of as a stone of reconciliation.

HEALING PROPERTIES: Wearing or holding Rose Quartz helps to heal all aspects of the heart. This stone emits strong vibrations of love. It's a powerful ally when you want to attract a new relationship, love yourself more, or heal from past hurts. By tapping into the energy of the divine feminine, Rose Quartz will restore faith, compassion, harmony, and balance in all matters of the heart.

KEEPING THE LOVE ALIVE

Time heals. As Timmi healed herself and developed her own self-love, her relationship with her husband, Jim, began to rekindle and heal as well. Instead of seeing him as imperfect, she realized that they were two perfectly imperfect people who still loved each other. But how were they going to deal with the anger and trust issues that existed between them? Would they ever be able to forgive one another? It started with communication, as well as ownership of their own demons.

They took the time to honestly express their feelings, and in doing so, the demons that had once haunted them became smaller and smaller. It didn't happen overnight, of course, just as their problems didn't develop overnight. It took commitment, faith, and patience on both their parts, and it's still a work in progress. But that's what makes successful, long-lasting relationships—growing together and regularly recommitting to one another.

KEEPING THE LOVE ALIVE RITUAL

TIME FRAME:
*10 days or as long as it takes for both
partners to communicate their feelings*

Most often in relationships, we disconnect from each other because we hold our feelings inside and don't express them. When a relationship starts running on empty, how do you refill the empty tank with love? One huge secret is to accept your partner as they are. This isn't always an easy task, but it's the key to keeping the love alive.

Sometimes words can be taken the wrong way, but expressing your truth with authenticity, compassion, and love can bring people back together with renewed respect and commitment. The Keeping the Love Alive Ritual helps you express your truth, clear the air, and share with your partner what you most appreciate about them. This helps to uplift the relationship and refill it with love. The ritual allows each person to feel heard and respected and is designed to open your hearts so that you can communicate with love.

Practice this ritual every day for 10 days to foster a deeper connection to each other. Some couples like to do this as a daily ritual to maintain their loving connection.

One person should hold the Rhodonite, and the other the Kambaba Jasper. Pink and green are the colors of the heart chakra. The colors are not gender specific, so just choose the one you feel most attracted to. They represent the energies of yin and yang, which are part of every relationship, whether between different or same genders.

WHAT YOU'LL NEED:

1 Rhodonite stone that fits in the palm of your hand for forgiveness, compassion, and releasing of fear

1 Kambaba Jasper stone that fits in the palm of your hand for overcoming fears, opening the heart, and restoring balance

1 sage stick

1 feather

1 abalone shell or fireproof container to catch ashes from the sage

RITUAL STEPS:

1. Sage your environment, and cleanse your crystals (page 22).
2. Find a comfortable spot where you and your partner can sit back to back. In this way, you create a safe space so that each of you can be vulnerable and speak your truth without having to look each other in the eyes, while still maintaining a connection through the touch of your backs.
3. Each person holds a crystal in their hand, over their heart. Close your eyes, and take 3 deep breaths. Aloud or in your head, say the following: *"I ask that the highest vibration of love and light connect with my highest self to clear all unwanted energy and any previous programming. I command this crystal to hold the intention of honesty, respect, and appreciation. Thank you, thank you, thank you."*
4. As you hold the stones in your hands, sitting back to back, take turns freely sharing out loud 3 things that you find frustrating, annoying, or disappointing about your relationship. By sharing what bothers you and not holding it in, less resentment will build up, and you'll allow space for more love between you.

This is the time to get it all out, but be mindful of the way you use your words. Focus on how you feel when something happens (or doesn't happen) within the relationship. Avoid placing blame. Take full ownership of your personal feelings by starting with "I feel," and being careful to use *I* rather than *you*. Stating your feelings about a situation from your perspective helps prevent the other person from becoming defensive and shutting down.

5. When you're both finished sharing, make sure each partner acknowledges hearing what was said. You can say something as simple as, "I hear you."

6. Take note how it feels to hear what your partner says. Notice if it might be hard to listen and not interrupt. Remember that this is how your partner feels, so even if their words or actions weren't intended to make you feel that way, the feelings exist. So just listen. Take a few moments to process what has been shared before moving to the next step.

7. Continue to hold the stones in your hands as you shift positions and face one another. Look in your partner's eyes, and focus on the good in the other person. Say 3 things out loud that you love or appreciate about your partner. If you're feeling very angry, it might be difficult to think of even one good thing to say. Make sure you choose something that's sincere and authentic, but it can be simple and mundane like, "I appreciate that you said 'good morning' when we woke up today." Recall all the things your partner does to make you happy. This will remind you why you fell in love in the first place. Use what you hear as encouragement to do more nice things for each other. To fill your tank back up with love, you must start with celebrating the positive aspects of your relationship and appreciating each other for who you are.

8. After each person has spoken their truth, sage the space again to clear the energy of the room.

9. Each person should place their stone on a nightstand while they sleep.

10. The following morning of each day of the ritual, place your crystals out in the Sun for at least 4 hours to cleanse and recharge them.

11. The next time you perform the ritual, change stones. The person who held the Kambaba Jasper should hold the Rhodonite and vice versa.

HOW TO MEND A BROKEN HEART

Healing from hurts can take a long time, but you can help the process move quickly with Rainbow Obsidian. Place a heart-shaped Rainbow Obsidian on your chest, close your eyes, and deepen your breath. This stone forces you to look in the mirror and see what parts of yourself you've projected on to others. You won't be able to blame anyone else for relationship issues, and you'll pinpoint what causes your heartache.

Now, think about the relationship that ended, and ask yourself, *What lesson was this person brought into my life to teach me?* Remember that in order to heal, you have to let go of resentment and move toward forgiveness.

Really dig deep to discover the lessons. Maybe it was about boundaries, independence, or confidence. How have you grown since the relationship ended?

Once you discover what this person was meant to show you, the way you see them will shift. Then forgiveness will be easier, and you can put the relationship in the past so that you can welcome in both your best self and your best partner.

"Love is not something we give or get;
it is something that we nurture and grow."

— BRENÉ BROWN,
researcher, storyteller, and
#1 New York Times best-selling author

CHAPTER 9

BABY MAKES THREE

CRYSTALS FOR FERTILITY, PREGNANCY, MISCARRIAGE, AND BIRTH

"There are no two pregnancies, births or babies that are the same. Everyone's journey into motherhood is completely different and one of a kind."

— LORI BREGMAN,
doula, life coach, and author of The Mindful Mom-to-Be

I GOT PREGNANT ON MY WEDDING NIGHT. YEP, I'M THAT GIRL. MY MOM WANTED TO BE A GRANDMA, AND SINCE I WAS 33 WHEN I "FINALLY GOT married," she was beyond ready for a grandbaby. Wise woman that she is, she decided to take things into her own hands by being sneaky with some crystals. She used to be a clothing designer, so she naturally asked me if she could make my wedding dress. But while making the dress, she decided to handsew hundreds of Moonstones and other crystals into it. She told me that it would give the dress a magical energy that would "sparkle." I didn't put two and two together until I found out that I was pregnant and realized that she had chosen Moonstone because it's the stone of fertility.

On top of that, my wedding band had 11 healing gemstones from different parts of the world. When my husband picked up the ring from the jeweler, he was warned that we would need to take extra precautions if we didn't want to become pregnant. My wedding ring had been created under a very powerful Full Moon, and it was extremely fertile. Between my mom's efforts and the energy of the ring, my destiny was set. I gave birth to my son, Orion, nine months after my wedding day.

The universe had another plan for me when it came to getting pregnant with my second child. It wasn't nearly as simple as wearing Moonstones. This time I wanted to get pregnant, but nothing seemed to work. I tried everything.

I worked with a healer who educated me on proper nutrition. She performed energy healing on me twice a month to release energy stuck in my second chakra. I had specific bath rituals

with herbs, and I made myself three crystal belts—one with Moonstone and Larimar; one with Moonstone, Ruby, and Chrysoprase; and one with Carnelian, Garnet, and Turquoise—all with the intention of aiding my fertility in different ways.

My daily mantra was to be patient, as everything happens in due time, but I began to wonder if I would ever be able to conceive another child.

A big shift happened when my husband, Jason, and I went to the Esalen Institute, a healing center in Big Sur, California, where we could come together as a couple and consciously make the time, space, and love needed to conceive. While in Big Sur, a mystical woman told us that if we found a natural circle of redwood trees, we should walk into the middle of them and pray. When we were on a hike later in our stay, it was as if a beam of light guided us. We found the redwood trees, perfectly and naturally standing in a circle. We held hands in the center as we prayed out loud to God, the trees, and each other for a baby.

While in Big Sur, we also created a baby vision board, which required us to open up about what new energy we wanted in our relationship. After our trip, I felt lighter and freer because I had let go and surrendered. I was 100 percent okay with whatever God had in store for me.

Well, just five days later, I found out I was pregnant again. My body and mind were healed, and our prayers were answered. This time I gave birth to my daughter, Sofia Rose.

CONSCIOUS CONCEPTION RITUAL

TIME FRAME: *5 to 10 minutes daily for 15 days, beginning on a New Moon*

A wise woman once told me that our children are our teachers. They pick us, not the other way around. We have to embody the energy a baby wants and needs in his or her future life. Conscious conception of a child—whether through the union of you and your partner or through adoption or surrogacy—is one of the most sacred experiences that life provides. In order to consciously create space for new life, your intentions and actions must work in harmony.

Invoking and co-creating new life is a beautiful spiritual and creative process that can't be scheduled, rushed, or done methodically. This journey is about creating the unconditional love needed for a child to come into your life.

When you and your partner are ready to consciously conceive, deeply connect with each other through this crystal ritual. To best connect with the fertile energy of the Moon, start the ritual during a New Moon, which symbolizes the birth of something new. It's the ideal time to plant new seeds and set new intentions, so it's key to start the ritual during this time period. The Moon will continue to grow for approximately 14 days until it reaches its full expression as the Full Moon.

In our experience, couples who begin their Conscious Conception Ritual during the New Moon cycle and continue to connect with each other through the Full Moon have the best results. The process is different for everyone, but you can use this ritual as a starting point for generating the energy you need to consciously conceive. Then you can add whatever feels right to you as a couple, whether it's taking a vacation, planning a romantic date, or simply spending time together mindfully.

Of course, we can't promise that you'll conceive after this ritual. It's about uniting your intention as a couple and creating a sacred space for conception to happen. Often, unvoiced fears, the need for everything to happen on a schedule, or becoming too methodical about the process will block a couple's ability to conceive. The ritual may help you to alleviate those emotional blockages and restore conception to its true state of abundant love between partners.

WHAT YOU'LL NEED:

1 Moonstone that fits in the palm of your hand to carry the energy of being open to receive

1 Carnelian stone that fits in the palm of your hand to carry the energy of action and moving forward

1 sage stick

1 feather

1 abalone shell or fireproof container to catch ashes from the sage

RITUAL STEPS:

1. Sage your environment, and cleanse your crystals (page 22).
2. Together as a couple, gather your crystals, holding them in your hands. One person should hold the Moonstone and the other the Carnelian; choose whichever you're the most attracted to. Find a comfortable place to sit together either outside under the Moon or inside in a space that feels sacred to you both.
3. Hold the crystals in your hands, close your eyes, and take 3 deep breaths. Aloud or in your head, say the following: *"We ask that the highest vibration of love and light connect with our highest selves to clear all unwanted energy and any previous programming. We command these crystals to hold the intention of being blessed with a healthy baby. We are ready to be loving, caring, and conscious parents. Thank you, thank you, thank you."*
4. After you've programmed your crystals, take this time to talk to each other about this intention. Talk about how life will look, feel, and change when you have a baby. Talk about how this makes you both feel, voicing your excitement, fears, and anything you may be struggling with.
5. Close your eyes, and visualize your intention coming to life. Picture it in your mind's eye, and experience it with your senses—the smells, sounds, and feelings of holding a baby.
6. When you're finished visualizing, place your crystals together on a nightstand. Your crystals will hold the energy of your united intention.
7. For the next 14 days, through the Full Moon, repeat steps 2 through 6.

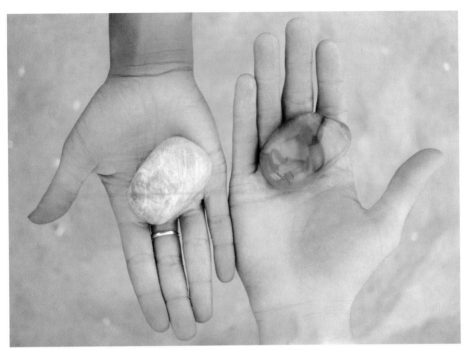

MORE STONES TO HELP YOU CONCEIVE

To amplify your conceiving energy, you can also add these stones to your ritual if you feel called to do so. They help to increase fertility by releasing emotional blockages:

- **GARNET** to stimulate the flow of energy and movement

- **FLUORITE** to increase libido

- **ROSE QUARTZ** to foster unconditional love and self-love

- **RHODONITE** to heal emotional wounds

- **CHRYSOPRASE** to open yourself up to receive

CRYSTAL SECRET FOR FERTILITY

To further increase fertility, wear a gemstone belt around your bare belly so that it touches your skin. Make the belt with flat Moonstones, Rubies, Carnelians, Citrines, and Chrysoprases.

Moonstone

WISDOM KEEPER:
DESTINY MAKER

COLOR: Opalescent, ranging from colorless to white

ORIGIN: Found in many locations, including Australia, Brazil, Burma, India, Madagascar, Mexico, Sri Lanka, and the U.S.

HISTORY AND LORE: Moonstone has the reputation of being the stone of fertility. It's aligned with the energy of the Moon, and thus is connected to a woman's cycle. It has been used as a symbol of love and clarity since the Middle Ages. Indian astrologers believe having a Moonstone is a way to befriend the Moon. Holding Moonstones under the Full Moon is thought to make you feel connected to the universal rhythms of life.

HEALING PROPERTIES: The milky radiance of this crystal represents tenderness, and is believed to bring lovers closer together. Moonstone is a magical stone that connects you to your divine feminine and inner goddess. It helps you unlock the energy of the Moon that resides within you, thereby keeping you in a more balanced state.

THE PAIN OF MISCARRIAGE

During the time between having Orion and trying to conceive Sofia Rose, I got pregnant but lost the baby after three months. Every day I cried alone, feeling ashamed. I blamed myself for not being able to hold the baby in my body. I questioned everything in my life, from the foods I ate to my work schedule to my mental state. Each day I became more and more depressed, feeling as though a very dark cloud had landed on my heart and was never going to go away.

Several months later, my mom shared a story with me. She looked me in the eyes and said, "Remember when Grandma died, and I was overwhelmed with grief and cried for months? One day you looked at me and said, 'Mom, if you don't stop crying about Grandma, she'll never be free to rest and be in peace. She needs to know that you're strong enough to let her go.'" My mom then paused. "That's still the best advice anyone has ever given me."

That was exactly what I needed to hear to start the healing process. I also needed the help of a touchstone, however, so I reached for a large piece of Carnelian and held it in my hands. It's as if the crystal was saying, "I have been here waiting for you. Let's get your joy back."

After I took my son to school each day, I would head to YogaWorks in Santa Monica, where I would place a piece of Carnelian on my mat as I breathed, sweated, and cried. I had bottled up all my shame, not telling anyone I had miscarried, and blocking myself from others. I let grief fill my body, but as I worked with the Carnelian, it helped me release that emotion. I did this five days a week until all my tears moved out of me.

At that point, I was raw enough that when someone asked me how I was, I actually told them about the miscarriage. I said it out loud. When I finally released that trapped energy, the healing started. I found other women who had also gone through a miscarriage, and I suddenly had a community I could lean on as I healed.

MISCARRIAGE RITUAL

TIME FRAME:
21 minutes daily for 40 days

Often when we're grieving, we ignore the things we know we need to do. It took months for me to reach for a crystal, even though I knew it was exactly what I needed. My wake-up call was my mother reminding me of the words I had offered to her.

If you've also been through a miscarriage or a stillbirth and have yet to heal, use this moment right now as your wake-up call. Stop avoiding what you know you need to do, and allow yourself to heal.

It's important to do this Miscarriage Ritual for 40 days straight. (For the significance of the 40 days, see page 18.) If you miss a day, you must start back on day 1. The time investment is 21 minutes a day. If you can't commit to 21 minutes a day for yourself, how can you expect to heal? Nobody can do this for you. It's up to you, but you do have the power to start the healing process. It will just take a daily investment of time to nurture your soul. You're worth it!

WHAT YOU'LL NEED:

---

1 Carnelian crystal to reignite joy and passion

1 Black Onyx crystal to release grief and pain

1 Smoky Quartz crystal to let go of the past and reconnect to yourself

1 Rainbow Obsidian crystal to allow yourself to bring the truth to the surface

1 timer

1 journal

1 pen

1 bar of lavender soap

1 sage stick

1 feather

1 abalone shell or fireproof container to catch ashes from the sage

RITUAL STEPS:

---

1. Sage your environment, and cleanse your crystals (page 22).
2. After cleansing them, hold the crystals in your hands, close your eyes, and take 3 deep breaths. Aloud or in your head, say the following: *"I ask that the*

highest vibration of love and light connect with my highest self to clear all unwanted energy and any previous programming. I command these crystals to hold the intention of letting go, healing, and releasing. Thank you, thank you, thank you."

3. Lie down in a comfortable position. Place the Black Onyx and Smoky Quartz on either side of your groin, and place the Carnelian at your navel, creating a healing triangular formation of energy.

4. Remain lying down with this grid on your body for 15 minutes every night before going to bed. Healing is an ebb and flow process, so some days you may feel nothing, while other days you'll feel overwhelmed with emotion. Be patient with the process.

5. First thing in the morning, hold a piece of Rainbow Obsidian in your nondominant hand. Set the timer for 5 minutes, and start freewriting in your journal. Let all the darkest parts of your mind spill out onto the page. "Why me? Why did this have to happen?" Allow yourself to purge the pain, sadness, grief, self-loathing, disappointment, and anger about losing the baby. Get it out. Once the timer goes off, stop writing.

6. Now set the timer for 1 minute. Stand up, and start shaking your body. This is how you shake your energy field. Shake your hands, feet, and legs. Jump up and down. Shake off all the negative emotions in your aura. Move as rigorously as you can until the timer goes off.

7. Every day, carry the Carnelian stone with you. Connect with it when emotions begin to arise during the day. Connecting with its energy will help you know what to do in each moment.

8. Every day, wash your body with a bar of lavender soap. This purifies emotional cords of attachment and promotes mental clarity.

9. At the end of the 40 days, rip out all the pages you've written in your journal, and burn them in a fireplace, barbecue, or metal bucket. Watch all your grief and sadness go up in flames and become ashes. You no longer need to hold on to it.

10. Once the ashes have cooled, gather what's left, as well as the Rainbow Obsidian, Smoky Quartz, Black Onyx, and Carnelian, and bury all of them in the Earth. Ask your higher power to help you surrender the pain and forgive yourself for anything you feel responsible for. As you bury the stones in the soil, know that Mother Earth is taking your pain away.

11. Congratulate yourself for staying committed to your journey of healing. You've gained new insight about yourself through this process. You're wiser and stronger!

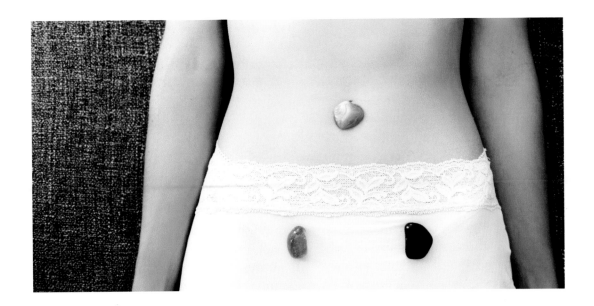

THE DISCOMFORT
OF PREGNANCY

While Timmi was pregnant with her first child, JB, she felt that the pregnancy glow had passed her by. One day, she was to have lunch with a group of our friends. She squeezed her belly into a trendy pair of overalls with a flannel shirt—something she would normally wear when she wasn't pregnant. But as much as she tried not to feel like a balloon, she had this crushing feeling: *I'm just not at home in my own skin anymore.*

During the lunch, she watched her girlfriends enjoy their fancy cocktails, while she drank lemon water. Her mind started racing. *Why are my ankles so huge? How am I going to handle missing out on all the fun for the rest of my pregnancy?* She hated the way she looked and felt, and nothing about pregnancy seemed right. Many women love being pregnant, but all Timmi could think was, *How*

am I going to enjoy being a mother if I can't stand being pregnant?

Unfortunately, for most women, these kinds of doubts, fears, and anxieties come up at some point during pregnancy. During the first three months, many women don't even share that they're pregnant. There's the fear that they might lose the baby. Then, once they clear the first three months, all the fears and anxieties about being a mother come to the surface. *Am I going to be a good mom? Can I afford everything this child needs? Will I ever have free time to myself or date nights with my partner again? I don't even recognize my own body!*

Emotions that we've never experienced before come right in the middle of this sacred time when new life is growing inside us. It's natural and normal, but it's unnerving. The pregnancy Soak in the Love Ritual will help you connect with your baby, your body, and your emotions in a heartfelt space.

SOAK IN THE LOVE RITUAL: A BABY BONDING RITUAL

TIME FRAME:
10 to 20 minutes as often as needed

WHAT YOU'LL NEED:

2 Rose Quartz crystals for unconditional love

1 cup unscented bubble bath

1 handful of fresh rose petals

OPTIONAL: *a candle, soothing music, Epsom salts (1 cup), essential oils*

RITUAL STEPS:
Just as a precaution, when pregnant, we do not recommend you sage during this ritual.

1. Cleanse your crystals by placing them out in the Sun for at least 4 hours.
2. Hold the crystals in your hands, close your eyes, and take 3 deep breaths. Aloud or in your head, say the following: *"I ask that the highest vibration of love and light connect with my highest self to clear all unwanted energy and any previous programming. I command these crystals to hold the intention of love, blessings, and happiness. Thank you, thank you, thank you."*
3. Place the Rose Quartz crystals in a bathtub filled with warm (not hot) water.
4. Add the bubble bath, rose petals, and any other essentials to create the perfect ambience for your bath.
5. Once you're in the tub, place one of the Rose Quartz crystals over your heart and the other over your belly. Breathe in deeply, and visualize yourself connecting with your baby, heart to heart.
6. Close your eyes. Breathe in self-love. Breathe out fear, judgment, and perfection. Breathe in confidence, trust, and love. Breathe out doubt, worry, and uncertainty. Breathe in excitement, blessings, and happiness. Continue this process for 10 to 20 minutes until you feel content, relaxed, and calm.
7. When you're done, sprinkle the rose petals on the ground outside to return them to the Earth. Recharge your Rose Quartz crystals in the Sun for a few hours so that they're ready for your next bath.

SETTING THE STAGE
FOR A SACRED BIRTH

When my daughter was 12 hours old, my doctor came into my hospital room to check on me. What he saw made him stop in his tracks. "Uh . . . is it okay to come in?" he asked. I was on my hospital bed with small stones outlining my silhouette. I had large chunks of Rose Quartz, Citrine, and Carnelian placed around the room. Roses sat on every surface. My essential oil spray had filled the room with the healing smell of lavender, and the mantra *om* was playing on repeat. My daughter was resting on my chest, and a woman stood over me, moving energy through our bodies.

"Sure," I said. "This is my Reiki master. She's just giving my daughter her first energy treatment to welcome her to the Earth."

The doctor didn't have to say anything. The expression on his face said it all. I can guarantee he'd never heard that before.

Most women have a bag prepared so that when it's time to go into labor, everything they need is ready for a comfortable trip to the hospital. While I had that bag, I also had a bag dedicated to my crystals and sacred birth space. It had everything I needed to ensure that my birthing space was a beautiful and loving environment for my child to enter.

Surprise, surprise, these were not the only things I had packed for my birthing experience. Additionally, I had prepared a cooler full of ice for my placenta after the birth. My plan was for Timmi to take it from the hospital to give it to my acupuncturist. It would be made into capsules to help balance my hormones after the birth and help prevent postpartum depression. Our plan was a success, but JB did notice it in the fridge and asked, "Mom, what's this?"

Timmi responded, "It's Heather's placenta. Don't touch it." I don't think she had to tell him twice!

SACRED BIRTHING RITUAL

TIME FRAME:
Will vary due to labor time

While you might not want to go to the lengths I did for my birthing experience, you'll definitely want to create a space for this beautiful moment and honor the sacred energy of childbirth. The crystals in this ritual will create a high vibrational space for the mother and baby to share the sacred time during the birthing process. Have the items ready to take with you when labor begins.

WHAT YOU'LL NEED:

---

4 Shungite cubes to seal the room with protection

1 Selenite wand to raise the vibration of your space

2 pieces of Black Tourmaline that fit comfortably in your hands to release fear, doubts, and pain

1 small Rose Quartz crystal for love

1 Hematite crystal for grounding

1 Amethyst crystal for peace and protection

RITUAL STEPS:
Just as a precaution, when pregnant, we do not recommend you sage during this ritual.

---

1. To make sure your crystals are ready and cleared, cleanse them by placing them out in the Sun for at least 4 hours before your projected due date.
2. Place all your crystals in front of you, close your eyes, and take 3 deep breaths. Aloud or in your head, say the following: *"I ask that the highest vibration of love and light connect with my highest self to clear all unwanted energy and any previous programming. I command these crystals to hold the intention of stability, grounding of excess energy, and inner peace. Thank you, thank you, thank you."*
3. For protection, place a Shungite cube in each corner of the room.
4. Place the Amethyst under your birthing bed to hold the space for peace and protection.

5. Place the Selenite on the table in front of you to guide the baby out. Lori Bregman, our friend and doula, has noticed babies are drawn to its positive and high vibrational energy and will follow the energy out into the world.

6. During labor, place the Rose Quartz in a safe place next to the birthing bed to open yourself to giving and receiving unconditional love.

7. Place a piece of Black Tourmaline in each of your hands. Visualize the stones pulling out any fears, doubts, or physical pain.

8. Place the Hematite by your feet to ground your energy.

9. Bring whatever other sacred items you'd like to have with you. These could include essential oils, a vision board, a special music playlist, photos of loved ones, or symbols or images that represent your faith.

NEW BEGINNINGS

Timmi had just given birth to her second son, Will, and he was in his "coming home onesie" as he nestled in her arms. Timmi's older son, JB, was playing in his room when she brought Will into their home for the first time. She lowered Will down so that JB could see him, and in a split second, JB wound up his arm and smacked Will across the face.

Timmi immediately burst into tears, in horror that her precious two-day-old son had just been hit in the face by his brother. She wrapped her arms even more tightly around her crying baby.

Timmi understood that JB couldn't completely process what was happening. After all, he'd been the one and only for two and a half years. She was thankful that her mother and grandmother were there to lend the extra support she and JB needed. Four generations got through a difficult time together.

It's with moments like these that we realize as mothers the sacredness of the first year of a baby's life. It's the beginning of your infinite relationship with your child. Your heart lives outside your body because you love your baby so much and want to nurture and protect them from harm and suffering. It's during this time that you have the ability to create a sacred and spiritual relationship with your child.

While you won't always be able to protect your baby from suffering, you can show them what unconditional love feels like and develop a bond so strong that you're able to openly share the ups and downs of life together.

NEW BEGINNING RITUAL

TIME FRAME: *40 days as needed*

Giving birth is a life-altering experience that's both profound and intense. It's important to take time to adjust to this new life so that you can heal and bond with your new baby. Many ancient cultures believe that the first 40 days are when a mom must strive to adjust to motherhood and establish a safe and protected environment for the baby to adjust to being out of the womb.

This New Beginnings Ritual will assist in keeping your environment cleansed and harmonious so that you can stay focused on bonding with your baby, while also staying present and connected with any other children you have.

This ritual is about creating a high vibrational and protective environment for your family to bond. Within this space, it's important to call on your partner, family, and tribe of friends to lighten your load by bringing you meals or helping with family and household responsibilities. This time period is about surrendering what you can so that your time is spent with your new baby. If you have other children, remember that this is a transitional time for them as well. Call in your patience, and practice this mantra: *Breathe and take it one day at a time!*

WHAT YOU'LL NEED:

1 small Jasper stone for grounding energy (a stone small enough to fit into the opening of a glass spray bottle)

1 small Black Onyx stone for protection (a stone small enough to fit into the opening of a glass spray bottle)

1 small Blue Lace Agate stone for harmony (a stone small enough to fit into the opening of a glass spray bottle)

3 Celestite crystals for one windowsill in each room to bring a high vibrational, calming, and uplifting energy

1 4-ounce glass spray bottle that is blue or amber in color (glass is recommended rather than plastic because plastic's toxins can seep into the contents of your spray)

Spring or distilled water

RITUAL STEPS:

1. Cleanse your crystals by placing them out in the Sun for at least 4 hours.
2. Hold the crystals in your hands, close your eyes, and take 3 deep breaths. Aloud or in your head, say the following: *"I ask that the highest vibration of love and light connect with my highest self to clear all unwanted energy and any previous programming. I command these crystals to hold the intention of harmony, bonding, and unification in the home. Thank you, thank you, thank you."*
3. Place the Celestite stones on the windowsills in the rooms where you spend most of your time, as well as in the newborn's room and siblings' bedrooms. Placing the crystals on the windowsills allows the Sun to hit them, sending their energy into the room. Celestite holds the energy of peace, and it also attracts angels into the environment.
4. To create an energy cleansing spray, first put the crystals into the glass bottle, the Jasper for grounding energy, the Black Onyx for clearing energy, and the Blue Lace Agate for harmony and joy.
5. Then, fill the bottle to the top with water.
6. To purify the energy in the rooms, use your spray throughout the day in the rooms when they're vacant.

"Stepping into motherhood can be one of the most healing, freeing, self-realizing, higher-level experiences of your entire life. It's the ultimate service."

— SOPHIE JAFFE,
*wellness guru, Philosophie founder,
and mama to Kai and Leo*

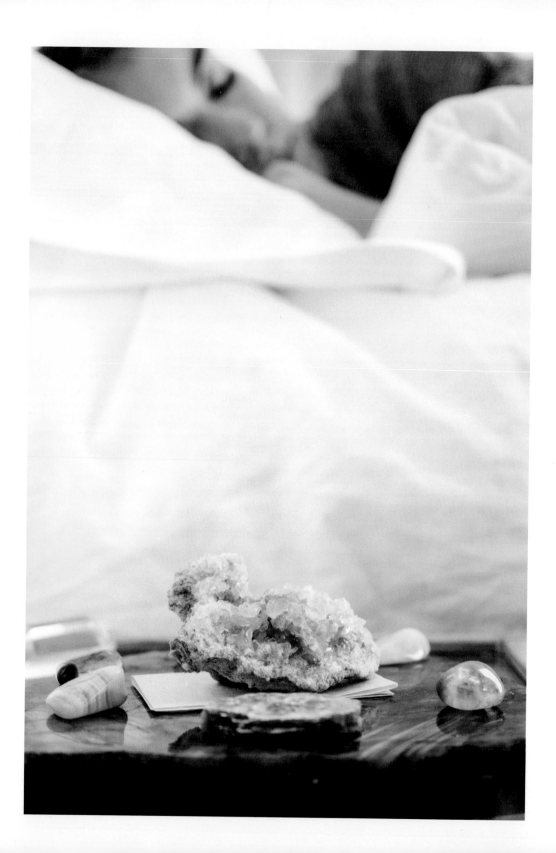

CHAPTER 10

SWEET DREAMS

TIPS AND TRICKS FOR
A BETTER NIGHT'S SLEEP

"Sleep is the deepest cleanse."

— KELLY LEVEQUE,
holistic nutritionist

PEOPLE OFTEN ASK ME, "WHAT ARE THE BEST CRYSTALS TO HELP WITH INSOMNIA AND ANXIETY?" I ALWAYS ASK THE FOLLOWING question first before I introduce crystals into the mix: Do you have a mirror, TV, or computer in your bedroom?

I have to admit—I've almost always been pretty lucky when it comes to getting a good night's sleep. I have a few secrets, however, that have helped me stay that way throughout most of my life. Without mirrors, TVs, or computers, my decor in the bedroom is very sparse to the point that I'm often startled by how barren it feels when I walk into it—especially compared to the other rooms in the house. My bed is placed in my best magnetic sleeping direction (try Googling *Feng Shui sleeping direction chart*), and it rests against a solid wall for support.

I always make sure to energetically cleanse and purify my bedroom every morning. I know

it sounds time-consuming to do every day, but getting a good night's sleep is that important to me. I've noticed that when I don't purify and cleanse the bedroom daily, the room feels heavy and dense, which affects my sleep.

So if you want to do more than envy my ability to sleep well through the night, get rid of those mirrors and screens, or at least make sure they're covered with a cloth while you sleep. Reflective surfaces, especially mirrors, double the energy in your room. This same energy bounces back and forth throughout the night, staying active while you sleep.

Call it a myth, Feng Shui taboo, or superstition, but some cultures believe that when you sleep at night, your soul leaves your body. If it sees its reflection in a mirror and gets startled, this is what results in restless sleep and nightmares. Some believe that mirrors need to be covered so that a dreamer's wandering soul doesn't get trapped in the mirror.

Now, I don't know about you, but I'm trying to do a lot of soul work in this lifetime, so it's more important than ever that I keep my soul intact. (If you don't believe this theory, try an at-home experiment by covering all the mirrors, TVs, electronics, and reflective devices in your bedroom for a week. Find out if you sleep better.)

My next question to people who want to alleviate insomnia is this: Do you have water or images of water in the bedroom? Once again, it could be a myth, but it's said that water in the bedroom has the potential to bring you financial loss. And of course worrying about finances is a sure way to keep you up at night.

My third question: Is your room cluttered? Bedrooms filled with clutter make your mind feel cluttered, which also makes it hard to sleep.

Fourth: Have you cleansed your bedroom with sage, opening all the windows and letting the sunshine in? If not, do it, and I promise it will make a big difference.

Finally we get to the crystals. Rose Quartz, Amethyst, Selenite, and Blue Lace Agate are your crystal allies for a good night's sleep. Place them on your nightstand, on a windowsill in your bedroom, or under your pillow. They create a very Zen, soothing energy.

So, that's my go-to formula, and it worked like a charm for years . . . until suddenly it didn't. I was wide awake one night at 1 A.M. as if it were 7 A.M. Something wasn't right. It was pitch black outside, and my mind wouldn't stop racing. *I need to get to sleep, I need to get to sleep. If I don't get to sleep soon, I'm going to be a zombie tomorrow.* This "mantra" continued to play in my head on repeat for the next hour.

I decided to scan my bedroom to see if something was off:

Bedroom clutter-free: Check.

Bed in best magnetic direction against solid wall: Check.

No mirrors or reflective surfaces: Check.

Bedroom cleansed and purified: Check.

Tranquil crystals under the pillow and on the windowsill and nightstand: Check, check, and check.

Ugh! My environment was holding the space for sleep, but my mind wasn't cooperating. It was time to look deeper, as I hadn't been sleeping well for weeks. I was stressed out about life—the world, politics, chemtrails, money, my family—it all seemed so overwhelming. Normally I could get it together, bring it all back into perspective, and be in the now. But that was no longer the case. And on that day in that moment after 1 A.M., my mind took me on a toxic ride of fear and negativity. I wasn't strong enough to make it stop.

I walked outside and grabbed a piece of Rainbow Obsidian that I was cleansing under the Moon. I picked it up and started to pray for help. I got on my knees with my head on the Earth, crystal in hand, and completely surrendered. I was under some false illusion that I could handle it all. I had forgotten my connection to a higher power—a source that was available to me at all times—but my ego mind was standing in the way of the connection.

I completely let go and started to cry. As the night sky shifted into the dawn of morning, I remembered that I wasn't alone and never will be. The Earth supported me, my connection to God (higher power) sustained me, and my heart was open to love and to be loved. When I remembered this truth, I felt freer. Suddenly, my anxiety and fears no longer had a hold on me. I stood up and walked back into the house with my Rainbow Obsidian, and went to sleep.

ROCKS IN MY BED

If you're not sleeping well, a number of factors need to be considered. Everything from what you're eating and drinking to medical conditions, stress, electromagnetic field exposure, life changes, depression, and more can affect your sleep patterns. Since we're talking about crystals, it's important to make sure that the energy of the crystals in your bedroom matches what you're working on energetically.

Here's what I mean: During the time I was having insomnia, I noticed that the crystals in my bedroom emitted a soft, tranquil, and loving energy. As my anxiety grew, however, I could feel myself spiraling out of my body. Yes, it was important to surround myself with loving vibrations and tranquility, but what I really needed right then were stabilizing and emotionally balancing stones that would ground me back into my body. I needed crystals that would help me breathe deeply and redirect my thoughts to the present moment. It was time to change the stones in my bedroom!

I picked up different crystals from my personal collection, and I could instantly feel the ones that resonated with me in that moment. I was magnetically drawn to the ones that felt nurturing, protective, and foundational because it was the exact energetic support I needed.

For two weeks I went to bed with tumbled stones surrounding me and physically touching my body as I lay there between the sheets. Yes, I'm serious—I had rocks in my bed. I placed a Rainbow Obsidian stone on my stomach, a flat-shaped Onyx on my lower back, and a bandage around my midsection to hold them in place while I slept. I then added small pieces of Nuummite, Black Tourmaline, and Shungite around my body and under my pillow. I placed a large Smoky Quartz crystal underneath my bed, put a piece of Hematite in both hands, and went to sleep.

Did my husband think that sleeping with rocks inside our bed was over the top? Of course he did, but guess what? It worked! I was finally able to sleep again. The mornings were a little tricky. I had to locate all the stones that had moved to different parts of the mattress throughout the night, but that was a small price to pay for sleep, glorious sleep!

GET BACK INTO ALIGNMENT RITUAL: FOR YOUR BEDROOM

TIME FRAME:
Nightly for 14 consecutive nights

Once I changed the crystals in my room, I was able to finally get into alignment and grounded back into my body. This ritual will assist you in doing the same. Feeling grounded and rooted in the energy of the Earth will promote a calm and peaceful state of mind, which in turn will help you get a good night's sleep.

WHAT YOU'LL NEED:

2 Nuummite stones for positive energy and protection

1 Lemurian Seed crystal for expansion

4 Peacock Ore stones to bring color and happiness into your life

4 Shungite cubes to neutralize the electromagnetic field energy and ground and stabilize the energy in your bedroom

1 small Clear Quartz point to activate your crystal grid

1 sage stick

1 feather

1 abalone shell or fireproof container to catch ashes from the sage

RITUAL STEPS:

1. Sage your environment, and cleanse your crystals (page 22).
2. Place all your crystals in front of you, close your eyes, and take 3 deep breaths. Aloud or in your head, say the following: *"I ask that the highest vibration of love and light connect with my highest self to clear all unwanted energy and any previous programming. I command these crystals to hold the intention of stability, grounding of excess energy, and inner peace. Thank you, thank you, thank you."*
3. Place 1 Shungite cube in each corner of your bedroom.
4. Place the 4 pieces of Peacock Ore on a windowsill where light can hit them.
5. Starting with the Shungite cubes, take the Clear Quartz point, and draw an invisible line connecting all the cubes, followed by the Peacock Ore, until you

have energetically connected them all. Think of it as "connecting the dots" like when you were a kid.

6. When you go to bed, place the Lemurian Seed crystal under your pillow and a piece of Nuummite in each hand.

7. As you lie there in stillness with your crystals, feel their grounding and calming energy, and be thankful for the good night's sleep you're about to experience.

8. When you wake up, place the Lemurian Seed crystal and Nuummite stones on your bedside table, but keep all the other crystals undisturbed in your room for 14 consecutive days.

9. After the 14th day, collect all your crystals, and reenergize them by placing them in the Sun for at least 8 hours.

10. After your crystals have been in the Sun, collect them, and repeat steps 1 through 9 of this ritual as often as needed.

MENTAL RESET

The majority of people are in some kind of pain—either emotional or physical. Most of us push unwanted feelings away when they become uncomfortable, telling ourselves that we'll confront them "later." We pretend to be okay when we're not, just so that we don't have to deal with unpleasant feelings. We may think we've forgotten these feelings, only to have them come up again just when we're trying to fall asleep.

If you're having trouble sleeping, crystals can help you reset your sleep patterns and sleep better. They're a physical form of the Earth's energy that you can hold on to and work with every day. They'll help you calm your mind, open your heart, and gently bring you face-to-face with any repressed emotional pain. Instead of running from your problems, pain, and emotional baggage, you can take the necessary time to mentally reset—dealing, feeling, and healing, which will lead to a good night's sleep.

Fluorite

WISDOM KEEPER:
THE RAINBOW KEEPER

COLOR: Ranges from colorless to purple, green, and yellow

ORIGIN: Found in many locations, including Brazil, China, Europe, and Mexico

HISTORY AND LORE: Fluorite has a long list of healing powers—as your healthy teeth might attest. Used to protect teeth, bones, and the immune system, the calcium fluoride that makes up this crystal has many practical uses. While there is little history on the metaphysical lore of fluorite, it has been used for decorative purposes since the time of the ancient Romans. Named after the Latin word for flow, Fluorite acted as a flux between metals. Today, Fluorite's ability to facilitate the transition from one state to another is used for more than just smelting.

HEALING PROPERTIES: Let fluorite guide you from a state of anxiety to one of tranquility by cleansing both your mind and environment. This is an absorbent crystal that will neutralize the negativity around it. Sleeping near or meditating with fluorite ensures mental clarity and harmony between chakras.

RELEASING PAIN, BALANCING EMOTIONS, AND RECOVERY RITUAL

TIME FRAME:

Nightly for 14 consecutive nights

Sleep is a restful time, but it's also a busy time for your body. It's vitally important that we get sleep. It's the time when our body repairs and restores itself. But some nights, sleep seems impossible. Whether you're suffering from physical pain, emotional pain, or a repeating loop of negative thoughts playing in your mind, this ritual will help you drift off to dreamland.

Placing an eye pillow filled with intuition-expanding Amethyst over your eyes at night will help you tap into a world full of possibility. These stones over the eyes also relax the nerves, calm the mind and third eye chakra, and balance the body—all of which work together to promote sweet slumber. Fluorite will soothe your nerves, and Apophyllite will raise the vibration of your space, allowing your emotional body to begin healing.

If you're suffering from physical pain and need some additional help to restore and repair a particular part of your body, drape a Shungite mat over that area. We have found Shungite to be one of the most powerful crystal healing tools for pain relief, arthritis, circulation, and physical healing. Due to the natural mineral and molecular structure of Shungite, it has a pain relieving and anti-inflammatory effect on the body.

NOTE: You can combine this ritual with the grid from the Get Back into Alignment Ritual: For Your Bedroom (page 169) to add grounding and stress-relieving energies to your space.

WHAT YOU'LL NEED:

1 lavender-colored eye pillow filled with Amethyst stones, Flaxseed, and Lavender to soothe and relax you

1 Apophyllite crystal to release stress and anxiety

1 Fluorite stone to alleviate worry and assist with emotional healing

1 sage stick

1 feather

1 abalone shell or fireproof container to catch ashes from the sage

OPTIONAL: *1 Shungite mat for pain relief*

RITUAL STEPS:

1. Sage your environment, and cleanse your crystals (page 22).

2. Hold the crystals and eye pillow in your hands, close your eyes, and take 3 deep breaths. Aloud or in your head, say the following: *"I ask that the highest vibration of love and light connect with my highest self to clear all unwanted energy and any previous programming. I command these crystals to hold the intention of letting go, emotional balance, and healing. Thank you, thank you, thank you."*

3. If you're choosing to combine this ritual with the Get Back into Alignment Ritual: For Your Bedroom (page 169), refer to steps 2 through 6 of that ritual.

4. Place the Fluorite stone under your pillow.

5. Place the Apophyllite crystal on your nightstand next to your bed.
   OPTIONAL: If you're using a Shungite mat, place it on the area of your body where you are experiencing pain.

6. When you go to bed, place the eye pillow over your eyes. If it falls off while you're sleeping, don't worry! Just replace it over your eyes if you wake up during the night.

7. Since you'll be using your crystals nightly, it's important to cleanse them at least every 14 days or as you feel is needed. Collect your crystals and eye pillow, and reenergize them by placing them in the Sun for at least 8 hours. (If you're combining the two rituals, cleanse all crystals in the Sun at the same time.)

8. After your crystals are cleansed, repeat steps 1 through 6 as often as necessary.

Amethyst

COLOR: Ranges from light to deep purple

ORIGIN: Found in many locations, including Brazil, Canada, India, Madagascar, Namibia, Russia, Uruguay, the U.S., and Zambia

HISTORY AND LORE: You're ready to sleep, but there's that thing you've got to remember to do tomorrow and that meeting you hope you're ready for, and *uh-oh*, here come the memories of every embarrassing thing you've ever done. Why does our mind do this to us, and how can we get it to stop? Calm the pre-sleep anxieties with one of the most spiritually relaxing stones in the crystal kingdom. It is said that the high priest of Israel wore Amethyst in his breastplate, and today Amethyst continues to be a symbol of spiritual achievement.

HEALING PROPERTIES: Allow Amethyst's energy of contentment to wash away the day-to-day stresses that keep you up at night. In working with the third eye and crown chakras, Amethyst indulges your intuitions. Your innate desire to sleep will take over whatever is blocking you from letting go. It's also a great crystal for those who struggle with turbulent sleep and getting a full night's rest. The positivity cast from Amethyst is a natural enemy to the negativity that causes bad dreams.

SLEEP IS THE NEW SUPERPOWER

Dreaming of the days when just hearing the words "Twinkle, twinkle, little star" made your eyes sleepy because you knew it was time for bed? Like triggers from our childhood, crystals are a natural sleeping aid from Mother Earth.

They contain a variety of mineral-enhancing sleep soothers within them and help you breathe a little more deeply, tapping into the inner peace you need to give your brain a much-needed rest. Placing crystals on a gemstone plate is a way to create a soothing and peaceful atmosphere in a bedroom and encourage a deep, restful sleep.

DRIFT OFF TO DREAMLAND CRYSTAL GRID

TIME FRAME:
Nightly for 14 consecutive nights

Create a crystal grid for your bedroom to fill the space with tranquil, peaceful, and positive energies, which promote sweet slumber and dreams. While dreaming, you may receive answers to problems, important messages from your subconscious, or a resolution of past events, helping you to understand why certain things happened. By keeping a record of your dreams through journaling, you'll find that specific dreams or dream patterns recur. Recognizing these patterns or messages can help you uncover the underlying meaning of your dreams and make positive changes in your life.

WHAT YOU'LL NEED:

1 Labradorite plate to induce a dream state

1 small Celestite cluster to bring a high-vibrational calming and uplifting energy

2 Lithium Quartz stones to release anxiety, which is amplified by the Quartz component

2 Lepidolite stones for tranquility and peace

2 Blue Lace Agates to release stress and anxiety

1 Selenite wand for clearing energy

1 Clear Quartz point to activate your crystal grid

1 glass bowl that can hold at least 2 cups of water

3 tablespoons of sea salt

1 small piece of paper to record your sleep affirmation

1 journal to record your dreams each morning

1 blue pen—blue is the color of truth. It's believed that you're more likely to retain information when you write it with blue ink.

1 sage stick

1 feather

1 abalone shell or fireproof container to catch ashes from the sage

RITUAL STEPS:

1. Sage your environment, and cleanse your crystals (page 22).

2. Place all your crystals in front of you, close your eyes, and take 3 deep breaths. Aloud or in your head, say the following: *"I ask that the highest vibration of love and light connect with my highest self to clear all unwanted energy and any previous programming. I command these crystals to hold the intention of tranquility, peace, and rejuvenation. Thank you, thank you, thank you."*

3. Place your Labradorite plate on your bedside table.

4. Place the Celestite cluster in the middle of your plate.

5. Create a circle of stones around the Celestite cluster in the following pattern: 1 Lithium Quartz, 1 Lepidolite, and 1 Blue Lace Agate. Repeat this pattern one more time until you finish making the circle around the Celestite cluster.

6. Write a sleep affirmation on the piece of paper, fold it up, and place it under your Celestite cluster. For example, your affirmation might be something like this: "I am at peace, sleeping soundly, and experiencing vivid dreams. Upon waking each morning, I feel rejuvenated."

7. Starting with the Lithium Quartz, take your Clear Quartz point, and draw an invisible line between the crystals on the plate to energetically connect each to the next. Think of it as "connecting the dots" like when you were a kid.

8. Place the Selenite crystal under your bed beneath where your head rests.

9. Fill the glass bowl with 1 cup of water per tablespoon of sea salt to absorb any negative energy that may be released throughout the night. This bowl should be placed in a corner of your room where it won't be disturbed.

10. Every 3 days, take the contents of the glass bowl, empty it into the toilet, flush it, and repeat step 9.

11. Place the journal and the pen on your bedside table so that you'll be ready to record your dreams when you awaken. If you prefer, you can record your dreams out loud using your phone or tablet rather than write them down.

12. For 14 days, immediately after waking, record your dreams. Don't worry if you don't remember much some days.

13. Cleanse your crystals every 14 days or sooner if you feel it's needed. Collect your crystals, and reenergize them by placing them in the Sun for at least 8 hours.

14. After your crystals have been in the Sun, collect them, and repeat steps 1 through 13 of this ritual to continue to experience a dreamy and rest-filled sleep.

Celestite

COLOR: Pale blue

ORIGIN: Madagascar, Mexico, and the U.S.

HISTORY AND LORE: The name Celestite comes from the Latin word for heavenly. While the etymology probably has more to do with this crystal's pale blue shade than its angelic lore, the divine energy of Celestite can't be ignored. It is believed to help you attract angels into your life.

HEALING PROPERTIES: Although it's a high-vibrational crystal, Celestite's energy is gentle enough to be soothing. It connects to the highest realms to permit serenity within your third eye, crown, and heart chakras. Communicate directly with guardian angels and the universe to ask for spiritual blessings. If you are experiencing stress from unfamiliar situations or difficult relationships, working with Celestite can encourage reconciliation.

"Dreams are today's answers to tomorrow's questions."

— EDGAR CAYCE,
the "sleeping prophet"
and the "father of holistic medicine"

CHAPTER 11

STOP SUCKING MY ENERGY

REMOVING NEGATIVE ENERGY FROM YOUR LIFE

"When in my treatment room, I try to steer all conversations away from gossip and negative thinking. Always remember, do not let anyone walk through your mind with their dirty feet."

— DAYLE BREAULT,
founder of Goddess of Skin

WHEN SOMETHING IS GOING ON IN TIMMI'S LIFE AND SHE'S FEELING UPSET, I CAN FEEL IT AS SOON AS she walks into the room, before we even talk, and vice versa. I specifically remember a day when Timmi showed up at my house, and one of her eyes was bloodshot.

"What's up with your eye?" I asked.

"I think I scratched it. Maybe if I lie down on the couch, it will feel better."

She looked so uncomfortable, and I felt sorry for her. But I immediately thought, *What if she has pink eye?!*

I quickly ran to look up the spiritual meaning of conjunctivitis, or pink eye, from my go-to book, *You Can Heal Your Life*, by Louise Hay. It said the cause of pink eye is anger and frustration at what you're looking at in life.

I came back downstairs, handed Timmi some eye drops, and asked her, "How did your day go? Do you want to talk about anything?"

She put the drops in her eyes and admitted that she'd checked her son into rehab earlier that day. (Now I could understand where the anger and frustration came from.) She was forced to address a heavy darkness that she didn't have the coping mechanisms to deal with.

She started to cry and didn't stop for a very long time. Her heart had burst wide open, and all the darkness, sadness, and anger from the last five years came raging out. She had been trying so hard to be a strong source of support for everyone else that she hadn't been allowing herself to feel. It was time for her to get real with herself, address the situation head-on, and begin to heal.

She finally realized that her eye was getting worse, and the drops weren't helping. So she went home to get some rest.

Shortly after she left, I felt frustrated and angry. I had taken her emotions on energetically. We are so connected that I felt her pain and sadness. I woke up the next day feeling depleted, so I saged the house. Then I got a call from Timmi confirming that she indeed had pink eye, but she had received drops from her doctor and wouldn't be contagious anymore. She thanked me for letting her vent the night before, as she felt so much better after getting it out of her system.

I was happy that she felt better, but that didn't change how I was feeling. Even after I had cleared my space with sage, I felt as if a truck had hit me. I curled into a ball on the couch, energetically drained, and shut my eyes, hoping a quick nap would leave me feeling refreshed.

The sound of the phone woke me up. It was Timmi, updating me on the story from the night before. The situation with her son had gotten worse. When we finished the call, I couldn't get her voice out of my mind. It continued to echo in my head all night.

The next morning, I woke up feeling foggy . . . and with pink eye! I was 100 percent energetically depleted. I turned to my husband. "I think Timmi's become my energy vampire. She's draining all my energy, and I let it happen! I forgot to put my protective 'energetic armor' around me. She needs my full support right now, but I don't know where my energy ends and her energy begins."

It wasn't helping either of us to be energetically corded together. We needed to "dis-cord" from each other's energy so that we could each reenergize.

I am sure that most of you have had a similar experience. Often we can get the most

drained from the people who are most important to us. Dis-cording from someone's negative energy does not in any way diminish the love you have for them. In fact, the opposite is true. The stronger and more grounded you are, the better you are able to support someone else. In this chapter, we'll show you how you can disconnect energetically in a healthy way, while still maintaining your relationships.

ENERGY CORDS AND YOUR AURIC FIELD

Everyone has an aura—an invisible electromagnetic field of energy that extends anywhere from three to five feet around the body. When something interferes with your aura, such as sound waves from a TV, EMFs from a computer, or even family and friends, it can throw you off balance.

Imagine this auric field is like a big, protective bubble. When you're feeling happy and joyful, your aura shines brightly. If you're feeling depleted and low-energy, your aura becomes dimmer.

"Cording" is described as the sharing of energy between two sources. It can also be thought of as the energy that connects two people. These cords can be positive when energy is shared equally, or negative when an imbalance occurs. An imbalance will disrupt your aura, causing holes or breaks in your protective bubble.

Anytime you feel drained or depleted after spending time with someone, it may be because they have unknowingly "corded" to you. If someone wants something from you, it can

even happen when they aren't in your physical presence.

For example, let's say you just broke up with a significant other. You can't stop thinking about this person even though you know they aren't right for you. Your relationship was unhealthy, and that's why you ended it. But now your ex is badgering you, trying to convince you to get back together. Even though you've broken up, you're finding it hard to detach. This is an energetic drain. It's time to "cut the cord."

Cutting the energetic cord is easier than it seems. Just recognizing that you're still feeling pulled in some way has already empowered you to take control. How can you prevent yourself from getting corded by someone in the first place? It's simple: by keeping your personal energy as clear and joyful as possible. The Cutting the Cord Ritual can be used daily to keep your protective bubble healthy and strong.

Q: I can't sage my space at work, so how do I keep negative co-workers or energy vampires away in a way that's subtle?

A: You need an Amethyst crystal (at least the size of your palm) and some fresh sage! First off, clear and cleanse your crystal. Second, give it the job of creating an energetic shield of protection from negative energy in your work environment. Third, get a small bunch of fresh sage from your local grocery store and place it in a small vase with water. If you can't burn it, you're still bringing that purifying energy into your environment!

CUTTING THE CORD RITUAL

TIME FRAME:
11 minutes, use as needed

Timmi and I practice healthy cord-cutting techniques daily. Not only do we interact with many people throughout our day, we frequently attach energy cords to each other unknowingly. When one of us is in a bad mood, the other one might begin to feel the same way. Although it's never our intention to drain the other of energy, it happens.

When you "dis-cord," you're not cutting people out of your life. You're simply removing any unwanted energy that they've transferred to you or vice versa.

This simple ritual will allow you to cut the energetic cord with anyone or anything that's draining your energy. After you cut the cord, you'll use specific crystals to send healing light to the spot in your protective bubble that might have been weakened. By using this ritual as needed, you are constantly maintaining a strong protective bubble and a vibrant aura.

WHAT YOU'LL NEED:

1 Black Kyanite fan to cut away any unwanted energies and repair any tears or holes in your chakras and aura

1 Clear Quartz point to create and activate a new energy field

A timer

1 sage stick

1 feather

1 abalone shell or fireproof container to catch ashes from the sage

RITUAL STEPS:

1. Sage your environment, and cleanse your crystals (page 22).
2. Hold the crystals in your hands, close your eyes, and take 3 deep breaths. Aloud or in your head, say the following: *"I ask that the highest vibration of love and light connect with my highest self to clear all unwanted energy and any previous programming. I command these crystals to hold the intention of release, healing, and light. Thank you, thank you, thank you."*

Step #5   Step #6

3. Find a space where you can comfortably stand with both feet planted firmly
   on the ground. Standing helps you to stay grounded and rooted with Mother
   Earth's energy. Make sure your timer is easily accessible.

4. Hold the Black Kyanite fan in your dominant hand.

5. Because energy cords often connect to the chakras within your energy field, it's
   important to address all your chakra centers. Starting at the base of your spine
   at your first, or root, chakra and ending above your head at the seventh, or
   crown, chakra, use the Black Kyanite like a blade, "cutting" it up the front of
   your energy body, along your chakra line. (Don't actually touch your physical
   body with the stone; you're cutting through the energetic body that emits from
   your physical body.) This will cut any cords that are connected within your
   chakras, sweeping away the unwanted energy that they carry with them.

Step #8

6. Starting at the first, or root, chakra, hold your Black Kyanite over each of your seven chakra centers for one minute each, finishing at your seventh, or crown, chakra. This sends healing energy to each of the sites where a cord was previously attached, repairing any holes or tears in the chakras and aura.

7. Place the Black Kyanite to the side after you're finished, and pick up the Clear Quartz point with your dominant hand.

8. Fully extend your dominant arm over your head, holding the Clear Quartz point with the tip pointing toward the sky, and sweep your arm in a clockwise motion down to your feet and back up, drawing a circle around you.

9. Close your eyes, and visualize yourself inside a ball of white and violet light. You should feel as if you have completely encircled yourself with a bubble of light. This bubble will act as your new, clean energetic field.

10. Repeat steps 1 to 9 regularly to dis-cord from any unwanted energies and purify your energy field.

SPIRITUAL HYGIENE

Have you ever walked into a space that looks clean and tidy, but feels heavy and dark? To keep our homes clean, we must mop the floors, dust the furniture, and scrub the bathrooms. But how do we keep our homes free of psychic dirt and spiritual disorder? With a good spiritual cleansing!

Negative energy is pretty much unavoidable. We all have it. Disagreements, harsh words, toxic thoughts, electronics, music with low vibrational frequency—all add up to stuck energy. This lurking, unwanted energy is similar to a layer of dust. It's trapped and has no way of getting out until you release it.

Just like dust, negative energy can build up over time. Lower vibrational energy can become heavy and dense, affecting your aura, mood, and the overall atmosphere of your home. It is important to clean your home both physically *and* spiritually after arguments, sickness, chaos, divorce, major life transitions, and even happy events with lots of people.

Smudging your house with sage, burning Frankincense, and ringing Tibetan bells are effective ways to spiritually cleanse your environment. All these techniques are simple enough to use daily. Every now and then, however, we recommend a deep spiritual cleansing. It's similar to a good spring cleaning and will restore the energetic vitality of your environment so that it feels light, clear, and vibrant. (For more about space clearing, see page 21.)

Black Kyanite

WISDOM KEEPER:
NONATTACHMENT

COLOR: Black

ORIGIN: Brazil and India

HISTORY AND LORE: Some say that the protector Archangel Michael's sword was made of a blade of Kyanite. Why? Because you don't mess with this crystal. The name Kyanite comes from the Greek word for deep blue, and this variety of silicate crystal is one of the most popular. All varieties of Kyanite, whether it's blue, green, or black, are considered strong conductors of metaphysical work.

HEALING PROPERTIES: Black Kyanite protects your energy field from relationships or people who feast on your positive vibrations, but offer nothing in return. Connecting with Kyanite's energy when your own energy is drained forces you to evaluate the situation. Once you know what you're dealing with, you can release that toxic negativity and raise your vibrational frequency once again. This crystal works with all the chakras to bring your energy field back into alignment. When placed upon your seven chakras, it directs its healing energy to repair any tears or holes. Black Kyanite clears out imbalances and energy blocks to restore a positive flow of energy throughout your body.

SPIRITUAL CLEANSING RITUAL

Will vary depending on the size of your space.
Repeat as often as needed.

As much as we try to avoid it, negative energy can still find its way into our space from time to time. Even our entrances and windows can act as openings for these energies to filter in from the outside world. This ritual will help you restore balance and harmony to your environment. The ritual has two parts: First, you'll physically and energetically cleanse your space. This will restore positive vibrations back into your home, place of work, or wherever else you spend time. Then you'll add crystals for an extra layer of protection. These crystals will keep negative, unwanted energies out as much as possible.

PART 1:

Cleansing Your Space

WHAT YOU'LL NEED:

1 large bucket filled with water for mixing your cleaning and clearing solution

1 pair of rubber gloves

Towels for physical cleaning

Juice of 5 lemons to purify, cleanse, and energetically ward off the evil eye

1 container of sea salt (at least 26.5 ounces) for cleansing and purification

½ cup of white distilled vinegar to cleanse and clear the energy

1 sprig of fresh sage to remove and clear out negative energy

1 Tibetan bell or singing bowl

1 sage stick

1 feather

1 abalone shell or fireproof container to catch ashes from the sage

RITUAL STEPS:

————

1. Add the lemon juice, 1 cup of salt, vinegar, and fresh sage to the bucket of water.

2. Set an intention for this solution to hold the space for cleansing and clearing the energy.

3. Place the bucket outside in the Sun while you prepare your space. (If there is no Sun that day, don't worry—your solution will still work!) NOTE: You may have to make multiple batches of the solution, depending on the size of your space; repeat steps 1 to 3 as necessary.

4. While your solution is outside being infused with protective energy, begin to prepare your space. Start by airing it out. Open all the curtains and windows, and let the natural light and fresh air fill the rooms. Sunlight has a clearing effect, and opening the windows will get the energy moving.

5. Go through your space, and move anything out of corners. This releases clogged, stuck energy that may be lingering in those spaces. Sage the entire space, allowing the cleansing smoke to reach every crevice and corner (page 23).

6. Walk through your entire space while ringing a bell or singing bowl, allowing its sound vibrations to break up any unwanted energy, making room for good, clean energy to enter (page 28).

7. Bring the solution inside, grab your towels, and put on your rubber gloves.

8. Soak a towel in the solution, and wring out any excess liquid. Clean all the doors, doorknobs, and windows. This clears the energy left by anyone who has entered the space, and it protects the area from the chaos of the world outside.

9. After you've finished, sage the rooms one more time.

10. Pour sea salt on the outside of your entrances along the thresholds to prevent unwanted energy from entering.

11. Repeat steps 1 to 10 as needed to cleanse and clear more of your space.

PART 2:

Protecting Your Space with a Protective Crystal Grid Pot

___

Now that your space has been cleansed and cleared of unwanted energy, you're ready to activate the protective component of this ritual!

WHAT YOU'LL NEED:

___

1 large pot (at least 8" in diameter) to hold the crystal grid

Rice (enough to fill the pot) to help absorb any unwanted energy

1 Black Tourmaline crystal to absorb negative or toxic energy and create a protective shield

4 Pyrite stones to repel negative energy

4 Labradorite stones to ground, protect, and repel negative energy

1 small Clear Quartz point to activate your crystal grid

1 sage stick

1 feather

1 abalone shell or fireproof container to catch ashes from the sage

RITUAL STEPS:

___

1. Sage your environment, and cleanse your crystals (page 22).
2. Hold your crystals in your hands, close your eyes, and take 3 deep breaths. Aloud or in your head, say the following: *"I ask that the highest vibration of love and light connect with my highest self to clear all unwanted energy and any previous programming. I command these crystals to hold the intention of clearing, protection, and repelling of negative energy. Thank you, thank you, thank you."*
3. Add rice to the pot until it's filled to 1 inch from the top.
4. Place the Black Tourmaline in the center of the rice.
5. Place the 4 Labradorite stones evenly in a circle around the Black Tourmaline (at the 12 o'clock, 3 o'clock, 6 o'clock, and 9 o'clock positions).
6. Place a Pyrite stone in between each Labradorite.
7. Starting with a Labradorite, take your Clear Quartz point and draw an invisible line between all the crystals in the pot to energetically connect each to the next. Think of it as "connecting the dots" like when you were a kid.
8. Now that your crystal grid is activated, place the pot by the main entrance of your home.
9. Leave the pot in its designated place for up to 6 months, or until you feel it's time to change the rice, repeating steps 1 to 7.

"I VANT TO SUCK YOUR ENERGY"

Have you ever felt squeaky clean from the inside out? This can happen after a good cry, when you've allowed all your suppressed emotions to bubble up to the surface and pour out. You may feel like you've hit reset for your mind, body, and soul. Your life might suddenly feel hopeful, and you may even be able to breathe a little deeper. It's usually around this time—when your guard is down—that "they" can feel and sense your light.

By "they," we mean "energy vampires." Energy vampires tend to show up when you least expect it. Yes, they're real, and they're everywhere! But these vampires don't want your blood; they want to suck your energy.

How will you know what an energy vampire looks like? At first they're normal-looking people who usually have the best intentions at heart. They can be a co-worker, neighbor, good friend, or a family member. On occasion, the energy vampire might even be you!

"Vamping" energy off others can happen easily and unintentionally, especially when someone is overly fearful, has low self-esteem or a "poor me" attitude, feels jealous, indulges in gossip, or is overly negative or angry. If your immune system and auric field become compromised due to stress, poor nutrition, or lack of sleep, it's also easier to fall prey to an energy vampire.

When someone feels powerless and insecure, they look for someone else's energetic light to draw from so that they can uplift themselves. Even though you can't see it happening, you'll feel its effects. Luckily, crystals are a powerful ally to shield yourself from negativity.

Black Tourmaline

WISDOM KEEPER:
FORCE FIELD PROTECTOR

COLOR: Black

ORIGIN: Africa, Brazil, Pakistan, and the U.S.

HISTORY AND LORE: Tourmaline comes in a wide variety of forms, energies, and colors, ranging from pinks to greens to black. Ancient Egyptian legends suggest that on its journey from the center of the Earth, Tourmaline passed by a rainbow and took on its beautiful array of colors. Many shamans of African, Aboriginal, and Native American tribes carry Tourmaline to protect themselves from danger.

HEALING PROPERTIES: Black Tourmaline is one of the most powerful crystals for protection and elimination of negative energy. This stone places an energetic boundary between you and others, so that you don't pick up on unwanted energies. When placed in the four corners of a room, Black Tourmaline seals the room with a protective shield. In this formation, the stone also assists in balancing out the energy and dispelling the lower vibrations of a room.

PSYCHIC PROTECTION POWER BANDING RITUAL

TIME FRAME:
Wear for at least 21 consecutive days

Have you ever noticed that some of your favorite superheroes wear bracelets or bands on each wrist? Well, now you can tap into this secret by wearing crystal bracelets that "band" you with protective energy. Black Onyx absorbs negative energy, while Pyrite repels or reflects negativity, making these a powerful duo for protection.

Wearing these crystals on opposite sides of your body not only creates balance *within* your energy field, but also protects you from psychic attacks, bad mojo, energy vampires, and even the evil eye. This ritual is a simple yet very effective way to use the energy of crystals to protect yourself daily.

WHAT YOU'LL NEED:

1 Black Onyx elastic bracelet to create an invisible, energetic shield around your body, absorb negativity, and protect you from unwanted influences

1 Pyrite elastic bracelet to act as a protective, reflective energy shield; its mirrorlike quality reflects back any unwanted energy to its original sender

1 sage stick

1 feather

1 abalone shell or fireproof container to catch ashes from the sage

RITUAL STEPS:

1. Sage your environment, and cleanse your crystals (page 22).
2. Hold your crystal bracelets in your hands, close your eyes, and take 3 deep breaths. Aloud or in your head, say the following: *"I ask that the highest vibration of love and light connect with my highest self to clear all unwanted energy and any previous programming. I command these crystals to hold the intention of protection, transmuting negative energy, and shielding from psychic attacks. Thank you, thank you, thank you."*

3. Wear your Black Onyx bracelet on your left wrist. The left side of your body is referred to as your most sensitive and "receiving" side. Banding your left wrist with a Black Onyx bracelet shields your receiving side from negative energy, psychic attack, energy vampires, and any other unwanted energy.

4. Wear your Pyrite bracelet on your right wrist. The right side of your body represents the energy you put out to the world and is referred to as your "giving" side. Since you're giving out energy from the right side of your body, you want to ensure that you put out positive, protective energy for yourself. Banding your right wrist with a Pyrite bracelet acts as a reflective shield, as its mirror-like quality reflects back any unwanted energy. By placing the two bracelets on your wrists, you have protectively banded yourself against negative energies and psychic attack.

5. Band your wrists with this crystal energy combination for at least 21 consecutive days.

6. Throughout this ritual, cleanse your bracelets as needed by repeating steps 1 and 2. If, at any time during this period, you feel that you've come under severe psychic attack, cleanse your bracelets immediately.

Pyrite

WISDOM KEEPER:

THE DEFLECTOR

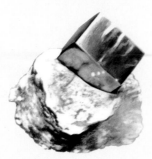

COLOR: Pale brass yellow

ORIGIN: France, Italy, Japan, Mexico, Peru, Spain, and the U.S.

HISTORY AND LORE: Often referred to as "Fool's Gold" because of its obvious resemblance to real gold, Pyrite holds a strong protective energy. Pyrite has been highly prized and used by wisdom keepers since ancient times. This stone will help attract wealth, abundance, and good luck. Because its mirrorlike quality repels any unwanted energy, ancient civilizations often wore it as a protective shield.

HEALING PROPERTIES: When you wear Pyrite, your aura is shielded against negativity and psychic attacks. It will also attract an abundance of good luck and positivity, and may even help you manifest gold.

"By releasing the relationships that drain my energy,
I create space to connect with people who light me up.

— ASHLEY NEESE,
breathwork teacher

CHAPTER 12

LIVING IN TUNE
WITH THE MOON

CELESTIAL CEREMONIES
FOR SELF-DISCOVERY

"I left a light on . . ."

— UNIVERSE

I WAS IN ONE OF THOSE "NOW WHAT?" PERIODS IN LIFE. I'D BEEN ON MY SPIRITUAL JOURNEY FOR A WHILE, AND EVEN THOUGH I FELT MORE open-minded and consciously aware than before, something deep within me felt disconnected. Maybe it was overload. I had become a sponge, reading every self-help book I could get my hands on. I had reached a turning point where I felt as if I'd gathered all the information on self-improvement I possibly could. Yet, instead of feeling clear from all the information, I felt more confused.

It was time to close the books. I couldn't go back to rereading the same ideas. Instead of intellectual stimulation, I needed to "just be."

I was also ready for a new teacher.

As synchronicity would have it, I met a medicine woman who invited me to attend a Native American sweat lodge purification ceremony. She held this event every month on or around the Full Moon. At first, I was hesitant. I had never been to a sweat lodge before. But since I'd been feeling so cloudy and energetically depleted, I thought a good sweat might do me some good.

The lodge was a dome-shaped frame, covered with canvas blankets, and had a hanging flap for the entrance. I was asked to bring an offering of sage, tobacco, and flowers. These were to be given to the people who kept the rocks hot on an open fire pit at the center of the lodge. We had the choice of wearing a bathing suit or nothing at all. I noticed that all 12 of the other women around me were naked—nothing but a towel wrapped around them. I felt self-conscious and uncomfortable, but everyone else acted as if it was no big deal. So I stood quietly in line and decided to do the same.

It was a cold night. I was freezing as we waited to enter. But the shivering stopped the moment I entered the lodge. Once everyone was inside, the hot rocks were added, the door was closed, and it was suddenly pitch black. I couldn't see anyone, but I could feel shoulders touching mine.

The medicine woman started singing Native American songs, and everyone joined her. It took me a few seconds to catch on, but I soon joined in, too. Each person took a turn praying out loud to the Great Spirit. The women bared their souls—sharing intimate and personal stories to release the pain and sorrow that had been lingering inside. When everyone had spoken, more songs were sung, and the door finally opened. Fresh air had never felt so good! My body was dripping with sweat—now I understood why everybody had chosen to be naked.

More hot rocks were added to the pit, and the door closed again. This round, we prayed for other people. It seemed as if it was getting hotter and hotter. Women cried and prayed, water was thrown on the hot rocks, and the steam filled every inch of the space. It was so hot that I could barely breathe. Finally the door opened again, and drinking water was passed around.

More rocks were added, and the process repeated. This round was for healing. It became hotter still. Sweat poured off my body. I felt uncomfortable and sticky, and I counted the seconds until it would be over. *Why am I doing this?* I asked myself.

At that moment the door opened, but we still had one round left. I didn't think I could endure it any longer. I wanted to leave. But I stayed, even though we were told this would be the hottest round yet. My mind was racing. How could it possibly get hotter?

I folded my body into a tight ball and decided to surrender to the heat. I felt the sweat pour out my fears, sadness, and negative thoughts. In the darkness, I could see my soul being purified.

The door opened for the last time. While I crawled out of the lodge on my hands and knees, I felt gratitude fill my pores. I was grateful for the Earth, the elements, the women who had shared the sacred space in the lodge with me, and mostly for my life.

Standing for the first time in more than three hours, I felt as if I was reborn. I was energetically lighter and in awe of the ground beneath my feet while I stood outside completely naked. I looked up and saw the Full Moon beaming down on me. I gasped! She completely took my breath away. Had she always been so luminous? I couldn't take my eyes off of her. I stood there bathing in her mysterious glow.

In that moment, I realized I had just begun a new relationship—with the Moon. For so long, I had been looking down at the Earth with the crystals. I now realized there was a new, undiscovered world right above me.

LUNAR AWAKENING

After this first sweat lodge, I attended one at every Full Moon for a year. Each one was different, but equally hard, liberating, and mind altering. The more I purified myself of my mental, emotional, and physical baggage, the freer I felt. During this time I was able to see through not only my physical eyes and ears, but my spiritual ones as well. I realized that beyond the mind, an entire world of spirit exists. We aren't separate from nature, the elements, and the stars above—we're all interconnected. I experienced it, saw it, and felt it.

When I was inside the sweat lodges, I developed a deep, personal connection with the Earth, but the moment I exited, it was the Moon that truly stole my heart. I sat under her beams for hours and hours afterward, absorbing her light and energy. I was so enthralled by her energy that I felt inspired to study the areas of life that are affected by the magnetic frequency of the Moon. These include plant medicine, a woman's reproductive cycle, the ocean tides, and even agriculture. Everything I learned made perfect sense. Our ancestors used to live completely in tune with the Moon for planting, hunting, and fishing. They lived in alignment with her seasons and cycles. They understood the importance of connecting with her phases and rhythms in order to connect with their own phases and rhythms. Somewhere along the way, we lost touch.

The more I stood on the Earth and connected with the Moon, the stronger the message became: The Moon had information to share with me, if I slowed down long enough to listen. I made a point of watching the Moon travel across the night sky. I allowed myself time for self-reflection. Soon I realized the Moon was reflecting back to me all that *I* could be—light, luminous, consistent, ever changing, and always interconnected.

MOTHER MOON
MANDALA RITUAL

TIME FRAME:
*Begin on a New Moon, and use nightly for
3 to 7 minutes for 28 consecutive days
or 1 Moon cycle*

This ritual allows you to align your manifestation process with the full cycle of the Moon. It gives you time for graceful self-reflection, discovery, and transformation while connecting to the Moon's divine energy. Working with your Mother Moon Mandala will allow you to work through the different parts of the Moon's cycle. You'll recognize that the Moon lives in a constant state of change—growing and releasing in accordance with the rhythm of the universe. As I had done in the sweat lodge, you will physically connect to both the Earth and Moon cycle as you work with your mandala each day under the night sky.

Although there are eight actual phases of the Moon, you'll work with the energy of four distinct parts of her cycle: the New Moon, the Waxing period, the Full Moon, and the Waning period. The New Moon marks the beginning of Mother Moon's cycle and is a time for new beginnings and planting new seeds. This is when you'll build your mandala. As the Moon grows, the Waxing period is a time for these new beginnings to bloom. Her energy slowly increases and intensifies while she brings in new energy, opportunities, and clarity. The Full Moon is the height of her power—her full expression. This period amplifies the energy you hold in your mind, body, and spirit. It also sheds light on what you no longer need. Finally, the Moon dims and moves to darkness. The Waning period represents a time of letting go. The Moon reaches the completion of her cycle, and it's a time of rest.

As you connect with both the Earth and Moon energy in this ritual, you're not only connecting with *your* natural rhythm, but with the rhythm of the divine universe around you. You'll feel the same expansive, cosmic connection to everything, and you'll know in your soul that the possibilities for you are infinite.

WHAT YOU'LL NEED:

Enough twigs to form a circle that's at least 40" in diameter

13 Basalt stones to represent 13 Moon cycles within a year (you can also use 13 stones you've found in nature)

Flowers as an offering for life, love, and beauty. Choose blossoms that resonate with the energy of the Moon, such as Casablanca lilies, gardenias, or jasmine.

A bowl of water for floating the flowers

1 sweetgrass braid to attract positive energy and good spirits

1 feather to represent spirit in your mandala and for saging your space

1 sage stick to be kept in the middle of the mandala for purification and to cleanse your space

1 Black Tourmaline crystal to represent the New Moon in its dark state, marking the beginning of the Moon's cycle

1 Moonstone crystal to represent the Waxing period of the Moon

1 Clear Quartz sphere to represent the Full Moon in its full expression

1 Labradorite crystal to represent the Waning period of the Moon

A timer

1 abalone shell or fireproof container to catch ashes from the sage

RITUAL STEPS:

1. Consult a Moon calendar (you can find one on the Internet) to find out the timing of the next New Moon.

2. On the New Moon, find a place outside where your Mother Moon Mandala can remain undisturbed for 28 days. Ideally, your mandala should be at least 40 inches in diameter. If you don't have a large enough space or don't have a place outside to create your mandala, you can create a mini Mother Moon Mandala on a tray that can be moved outside nightly.

3. Sage your environment, and cleanse your crystals (page 22).

4. Place all your crystals in front of you, close your eyes, and take 3 deep breaths. Aloud or in your head, say the following: *"I ask that the highest vibration of love and light connect with my highest self to clear all unwanted energy and any previous programming. I command these crystals to hold the intention of new opportunities, connection, releasing, and healing. Thank you, thank you, thank you."*

5. Create a circle with your twigs that is about 40 inches in diameter, or a smaller circle that fits on your tray.

6. In the middle of the mandala, place the 13 Basalt stones, bowl of water with flowers, sweetgrass braid, feather, sage stick, and any other offerings you may want to include.

7. If you look at your mandala as the face of a clock, place the Black Tourmaline at the 3 o'clock position to represent the New Moon.

8. Place the Clear Quartz sphere at the 9 o'clock position to represent the Full Moon.

9. Place the Moonstone at the 12 o'clock position to represent the Waxing period of the Moon.

10. Place the Labradorite at the 6 o'clock position to represent the Waning period.

11. After you've created your mandala, sit or stand in the center (if possible). Close your eyes, and visualize something new that you would like to bring into your life. The New Moon is the perfect time to manifest an intention, goal, or dream that has been on your mind. Set the timer, and allow yourself 5 to 7 minutes to become clear about what you want to manifest.

12. There are approximately 14 days in between the New Moon and the Full Moon, when the Waxing period occurs and the Moon builds. Nightly for these next 14 days, set the timer, and spend 3 to 5 minutes with your mandala outside under the Waxing Moon. Notice how the Moon changes and builds, paralleling your manifestation coming to fruition. Think about the steps you will take to create, manifest, and bring it to life.

13. On the night of the Full Moon, sit or stand in the middle of your mandala (if possible). Look up at the Moon, connect with its energy, and bask in its luminosity. This is a time when the Moon's power is at its peak and the time when you'll see your manifestation come to life. Do you see your dream being fulfilled? Set the timer, and allow yourself 5 to 7 minutes to reflect on this.

14. The final 14 days of the Moon's cycle, the Waning period, are a time for reflecting, letting go, and resting. Nightly for these 14 days, set the timer, and spend 3 to 5 minutes with your mandala outside under the Waning Moon, reflecting on your manifestation. Was there anything you would change? How could you prepare better for the next cycle? This is a time to nurture yourself, to feel appreciative of the energy, and to recuperate before you begin again.

15. When you're finished with this ritual, cleanse the crystals, and give back any of the Mother Moon Mandala elements you can to the Earth, such as scattering them in your backyard, a field, or a park. All other items, such as the sage and sweetgrass, can be used again. Repeat this ritual as often as you'd like to align with the Moon's cycle, always remembering to start at the New Moon.

ALIGNING WITH THE ENERGY OF THE NEW MOON

Many years ago, when I was first beginning my journey with Mother Moon, I was given a secret New Moon ritual from a wise medicine woman. She never explained the reasons behind this specific formula, but I have to say, after using it for over 15 years, it really works. Until this moment, I've never shared this New Moon secret with anyone—I didn't even tell Timmi until we sat down to write this chapter—but I felt it was time for everyone to experience its energy.

Labradorite

WISDOM KEEPER:
THE MAGICIAN

COLOR: Iridescent dark gray, blue, and white

ORIGIN: Canada, Madagascar, Mexico, Russia, and the U.S.

HISTORY AND LORE: Labradorite is thought to ignite sparks of neon to illuminate the path to your destiny. Labradorite is a stone of magic and curiosity. Its base color is dark gray, but when it catches the light, flashes of iridescent color appear. Legend says that some of the northern lights are held within Labradorite, giving it the colorful flash known as labradorescence. It's a tantalizing stone, one that takes you on a journey of color. It will bring light to the unknown of any situation. It's also a symbolic reminder to look deeper and from many angles, instead of taking things at face value.

HEALING PROPERTIES: Wearing or holding Labradorite helps you tap into a higher state of consciousness. It's a protective stone as well, so it will keep your energy body grounded, while allowing you to explore the expanded states of the universe. It boosts mental and spiritual power. Labradorite opens you up, forcing you to become aware enough to see your true intentions. Once your eyes are wide open, it will encourage you to find solutions.

NEW MOON WISHES RITUAL

TIME FRAME:
Approximately 11 minutes;
begin on a New Moon

The New Moon symbolizes new beginnings and a fresh start, making it the ideal time to make wishes, set new intentions, and plant new seeds. Watch them bloom and grow throughout the remainder of the Moon's cycle.

This New Moon Wishes Ritual allows you to honor the energy of Mother Moon while making wishes on the night of her new cycle. Creating a regular practice of setting New Moon intentions is a mindful way to commit to your dreams and goals. It will also allow you to stay in touch with her divine feminine energy. The power of writing down your intentions cannot be understated.

WHAT YOU'LL NEED:

1 copy of the New Moon Wishes Sheet on page 212

1 metallic silver pen or marker—silver is linked with the Moon

1 blue pen—blue is the color of truth. It's believed that you're more likely to retain information when you write it with blue ink.

1 Phantom Quartz point to bring spiritual growth and evolution

4 Lemurian Seed crystals to represent the planting of new seeds, wishes, and dreams

1 small Clear Quartz point to activate your New Moon grid

1 sage stick

1 feather

1 abalone shell or fireproof container to catch ashes from the sage

OPTIONAL: *Colored pens or pencils*

RITUAL STEPS:

1. Sage your environment, and cleanse your crystals (page 22).

2. Hold the crystals in your hands, close your eyes, and take 3 deep breaths. Aloud or in your head, say the following: *"I ask that the highest vibration of love and light connect with my highest self to clear all unwanted energy and any previous programming. I command these crystals to hold the intention of my infinite potential. Thank you, thank you, thank you."*

3. Consult a Moon calendar (you can find one on the Internet) to find out the timing of the next New Moon.

4. On the New Moon, grab your New Moon Wishes Sheet, silver pen, blue pen, and crystals, and find a comfortable environment outside where you can sit.

5. With your silver pen, go over the outline of the circle and the four Moons on your sheet.

6. With your blue pen, write up to 10 wishes inside the circle. Start with "Dear _____, [whatever fits with your belief—God, Higher Source, Angels, zero-point energy, or a similar entity]." Then list your wishes. It's very important to write your wishes within 24 hours of the specific time that the New Moon starts. (If you need help writing your intentions, refer to page 13.) OPTIONAL: Decorate your New Moon Wishes Sheet in whatever way you'd like. You can add colors or drawings inside or outside the circle, but your words must remain within the circle.

7. Add your signature and date at the bottom of the sheet as indicated.

8. Say "thank you" aloud three times to emphasize that what you're asking for already exists in the universe.

9. Fold your New Moon Wishes Sheet in half once and then in half a second time.

10. Place your wishes in an area where they can remain undisturbed for 28 days, or the entire Moon cycle.

11. Place your Phantom Quartz point in the center on top of your folded New Moon Wishes Sheet. With the points facing outward, place the four Lemurian Seed crystals around the Phantom Quartz at the 4 cardinal directions—north, south, east, and west.

12. Take your Clear Quartz point and draw an invisible line starting with the Phantom Quartz and moving to all four Lemurian Seed crystals until you have energetically connected them all. Think of it as "connecting the dots" like when you were a kid.

13. Leave your New Moon Wishes grid undisturbed for 28 days. At the end of the 28 days, on the night before the next New Moon, remove your crystals, and open your sheet. Reflect on your wishes, seeing which ones have manifested and which ones still need time to seed. Transfer those to your next month's New Moon wishes.

14. Cleanse your crystals, and repeat this ritual as often as you'd like to be in alignment with the Moon cycle, always remembering to start at the New Moon.

New Moon Wishes

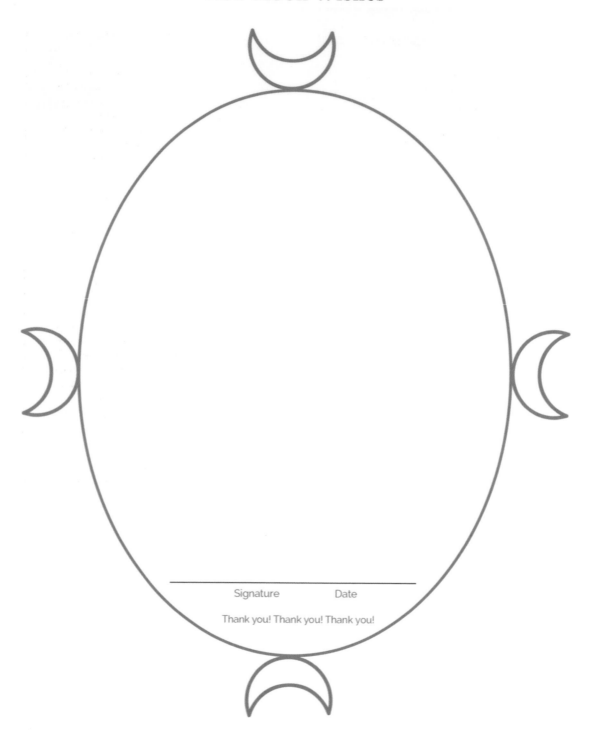

Signature   Date

Thank you! Thank you! Thank you!

Phantom Quartz

WISDOM KEEPER:
PUSH THE LIMITS

COLOR: Clear, colorless, transparent to translucent; can have various colors due to the different mineral deposits that they are composed of

ORIGIN: Found worldwide, including Brazil and the U.S.

HISTORY AND LORE: You may not see the energy of Phantom Quartz, but you'll certainly feel its presence in the room. *Muhahaha!* Actually, Phantom Quartz, also known as the ghost crystal, is nothing to be scared of. Like Casper, this is a friendly ghost. It gets its name from secondary crystal growths that haunt the crystal from within. These growths can be made up of minerals or can appear as another type of quartz, like Rose Quartz or Smoky Quartz. The crystal envelops these secondary growths, and creates the look of minerals or crystals floating within the primary crystal.

HEALING PROPERTIES: Not surprisingly, these crystals are all about growth. If you're feeling stuck in life, know that Phantom Quartz can help you to continue to move forward. The energy of Phantom Quartz can help guide you through a spiritual journey. It has the ability to receive and deliver messages to and from the universe. This is a crystal that can help you transition from one phase of your life to another. The transformational power of Phantom Quartz is a strong one, and the ideal energy for anyone going through a major life change.

RECLAIMING
HER FEMININE SPIRIT

While living in New York City in the 1990s, Timmi would often meet her friends from the garment industry after work at the trendiest spots. She and her friends would scan the room for the best table—one with easy access to the bar but close enough to a window so they could watch the action outside. The conversation was always the same, with each person trying to one-up the other about sales from the day and where they were traveling next to meet the big client. Business was booming in the garment industry at the time. If you were lucky enough to represent a hot clothing line, the money flowed . . . and Timmi's line was hot, hot, hot!

On one particular night, the bar scene banter and drinks couldn't drown out the replay of Timmi's day in her head. At that point, she'd learned to turn a deaf ear to her boss when he started yelling at her. He was constantly threatening to replace her if she didn't "sell, sell, sell." But the daily degradation was finally beginning to take its toll. Timmi was living in a man's world, because men owned most of the businesses that manufactured clothing. In order to master the game, she'd push aside her femininity to "play with the boys." Although she hated what it was doing to her, Timmi liked the lifestyle and money. Remember, the mantra of the era was still, "Greed is good."

Soon, though, the days turned into months, and the months turned into years. Timmi was beginning to wonder if this lifestyle was the best one for her. She'd made a promise to herself long ago that the day she became a "hardened bitch," she would get out of the industry.

On this night, someone ordered another round of drinks, followed by another and another. She kept up with her friends drink by drink, and joke for joke, while she quietly smothered herself in worry. Finally she excused herself to get some fresh air on the rooftop bar. Looking over the railing at the bright city lights, from the corner of her eye, she noticed a woman sitting by herself. This woman took Timmi's breath away. She had an inner glow that seemed to emanate from every cell of her being. She wore an elegant, flowing dress, and the wind billowed through her long, lustrous hair. She sat quietly. She wasn't trying to capture the attention of anyone on the rooftop, but she was doing it anyway. Yes, she was attractive, but that wasn't what was catching everyone's eye. It was her inner confidence and grace. It was her poise and femininity.

Timmi gazed down at her own clothes. She was wearing tailored blue pants and a jacket with a crisp white shirt and barely heeled shoes. Her hair was cut into a short bob. Was she purposely dressing like a man now, too? She realized that her confidence was at an all-time low. Looking over again, Timmi wondered if that woman would ever let herself be treated by her boss the way Timmi was being treated now. Would she endure the verbal and emotional berating that Timmi had been getting from him for the last seven years? *I'll bet she wouldn't*, Timmi thought.

Just then, a man came up behind the woman and kissed her neck. The woman smiled. It was a private moment, so Timmi quickly looked up at the night sky, at the Full Moon beaming down on her.

She cracked. A tear fell down her cheek. She'd conditioned herself to think of tears as a sign of weakness. But she didn't feel weak, she felt ready. This mysterious woman had reminded Timmi of something she'd lost touch with—her feminine spirit.

Timmi realized in that moment that she had indeed become the "hardened bitch" she swore she'd never be. She wasn't outwardly mean, but she'd grown out of tune with her own true self. Was all that money worth it? Nope. The lifestyle she'd been living had run its course. It was time to make a change.

The next day, Timmi gave her two weeks' notice.

ALLOWING THE FULL MOON TO FOSTER YOUR UNIVERSAL CONNECTION

On the night of a Full Moon, you can feel the height of her powerful energy. She's at her peak expression. It's a beautiful sight to behold. Learning how to harness the energy of the Full Moon connects you with your own internal rhythm—as well as the rhythm of the universe.

Spending time under the luminous light of the Full Moon will help you develop a deep connection with the world around you. It will illuminate your inner light and encourage you to let go of the separateness. It will inspire you to feel the oneness of the universe. If, like Timmi, you're feeling as if you've lost touch with your feminine spirit, the Full Moon is a wonderful time to start getting it back.

The energy of the Moon is available for everyone—not just women. Its luminosity, beauty, and grace shine upon us, for all of us to take in.

COSMIC CONNECTION
ALTAR RITUAL

TIME FRAME:
*2 days before the Full Moon for altar setup,
and 11 minutes on the night of the Full Moon*

On the night of a Full Moon, Mother Moon illuminates the Earth with her powerful light. Physically connecting with this energy by creating an altar outside in the moonlight unites the light of your soul with the light of the universe. Allowing yourself the time to connect with the lunar, Earth, and universal energies at once helps to bring all aspects of your mind, body, and soul back into balance. Your cosmic connection altar will hold the energy of wholeness and oneness, deepening your relationship with the cosmos to become more in tune with yourself. We are all made of the same light that lies within the Moon.

WHAT YOU'LL NEED:

1 small table, tray, or blanket to serve as the surface for your altar

1 Selenite crystal—named after the Greek goddess Selene, the goddess of the Moon

1 Moonstone to facilitate a deeper connection with the Moon

1 Labradorite crystal to connect you with the energy of the universe and cosmos

1 Unakite stone to balance masculine and feminine energies through the energy of love

1 Mason jar or bottle with a lid, filled with at least 1 cup of drinkable water

Flowers to be used as an offering. We recommend choosing white flowers that resonate with the energy of the Moon, such as Casablanca lilies, gardenias, or jasmine. Place them in a vase or bowl with water.

1 white candle to symbolize pure energy

A timer

1 sage stick

1 feather

1 abalone shell or fireproof container to catch ashes from the sage

OPTIONAL: *A pinch of glitter to represent cosmic energy*

RITUAL STEPS:

1. Sage your environment, and cleanse your crystals (page 22).

2. Hold the crystals in your hands, close your eyes, and take 3 deep breaths. Aloud or in your head, say the following: *"I ask that the highest vibration of love and light connect with my highest self to clear all unwanted energy and any previous programming. I command these crystals to hold the intention of cosmic connection, wholeness, and expansion. Thank you, thank you, thank you."*

3. Consult a Moon calendar (you can find one on the Internet) to find out the timing of the next Full Moon.

4. Set up your altar 2 days before the night of the Full Moon. This period of the Moon cycle is the most powerful. Find a place outside where your altar can remain undisturbed for 3 days (the night of the Full Moon plus 2 days before), and place your table or blanket in the space. If you don't have a space outside for your altar, you can create a mini cosmic connection altar on a tray that can be moved outside nightly.

5. Place the Selenite, Moonstone, Labradorite, and Unakite on your altar—4 represents the energy of foundation.

6. Place the flowers and candle on your altar. If you choose, throw a pinch of glitter onto the altar to represent cosmic energy.

7. Set the jar of drinkable water on your altar.

8. Leave the altar outside until the night of the Full Moon, and let the components absorb the Moon's energy.

9. On the night of the Full Moon, head outside to your altar, and light the candle.

10. Set the timer for 11 minutes, and sit in front of the altar underneath the Full Moon. Feel the moonlight filling every cell of your being. Feel the Earth underneath you and the universe above you. Release into the Earth anything that no longer serves your highest good. Feel everything shift back into alignment—your body, mind, and soul. Feel your soul and energy expanding outward, becoming one with the energy of the universe.

11. At the end of the 11 minutes, snuff out the candle, and drink the water from the jar. It has been charged with the energy of the Full Moon and the Sun.

12. Disassemble the altar within 3 days of the Full Moon. Return any altar elements you can to the Earth—such as scattering them in a park. Bring your crystals back inside to an area you'll see daily to remind you that you're one with the cosmos. All other items, such as the candle, can be used again for the next Full Moon.

13. Repeat this ritual as often as you'd like to remain in alignment with the Full Moon each month.

Unakite

WISDOM KEEPER:
LIVING IN THE NOW

COLOR: Green and pink

ORIGIN: Brazil, South Africa, and the U.S.

HISTORY AND LORE: Give your third eye 20/20 vision with the energy of Unakite. Named after the Unaka Mountains of North Carolina where it was first discovered, it is thought to assist in meditation by encouraging a sense of presence. It is also thought to release energies of the past, especially those that are toxic.

HEALING PROPERTIES: Free yourself of the negative energy of past mistakes or hurt, and live in a moment of tranquil understanding. Unakite will guide you to find your place of grounded power. It enhances your energy field by dissipating negative forces. Unakite is especially recommended for those attempting to move on from emotional pain, and for pregnant women trying to establish a connection with their baby. This crystal is helpful for anyone hoping to amplify their present spirituality.

"The moon drives your deepest feelings, the fine-tuning of your character, your instinct and intuition, your emotions and your reactions."

— SUSAN MILLER,
astrologer and author

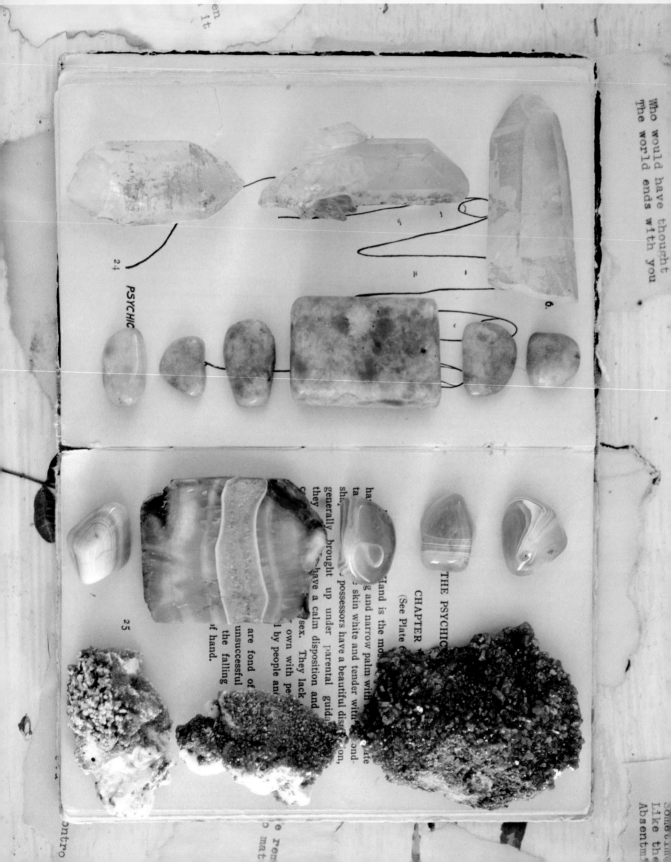

CHAPTER 13

YOUR CREATIVE SPIRIT

KEYS TO UNLOCKING YOUR CREATIVITY

*"Creativity is simply an expression of the self—
the highest self that is, the part of us that is pure
Source energy. And since we are all born as the
physical embodiment of this, not only is creativity
our birthright—but we are born to create."*

— RUBY WARRINGTON,
journalist and founder of The Numinous

I STARTED DESIGNING CRYSTAL JEWELRY IN THE YEAR 2000, AND MY FIRST NECKLACE COLLECTION WAS TO BE BASED ON NUMEROLOGY. I collected hundreds of strands of gemstones from all over the world. The first time I saw them all lined up together, I was amazed. Each strand glistened with light, energy, and beauty. I couldn't wait to get started.

But every time I tried to create a pattern, I stopped. The crystals were astonishing, but my designs were lacking vision and creativity. I knew I wasn't "in the zone." I kept trying to push through my creative blocks. Surely, something would emerge if I just kept at it, right?

Well, not exactly.

After endless hours with nothing to show for my best efforts, it was clear that my inner creative child had left the building. I was on my own. Did I mention I had a looming deadline hanging over my head? If I finished the collection on time, there was a chance that one of my pieces would be featured in a national fashion magazine. This was a huge opportunity. Our business was still very new, and Energy Muse was one of the only companies designing crystal energy jewelry at the time. Getting the magazine exposure would give us a large platform to introduce crystal energy to the mainstream. But I had absolutely nothing done—nothing.

I was getting desperate. I needed to act fast. There was only one thing left to do—immerse myself in orange. (The color orange inspires creative energy.) I ran to my room, threw on an orange T-shirt, put on Carnelian earrings and a Sunstone necklace, threw a Tangerine Quartz point in my pocket, and screamed, "Creativity, I demand you come back to me right now!"

Orange must have gone on a playdate with my inner child, because nothing but silence filled the room. There were no bursts of inspiration or sudden visions of beauty. There was only more and more . . . nothing. Until finally I heard the tiniest, saddest voice in the room—mine—tell me the truth: My creativity took orders from no one. And she wouldn't be back until she was good and ready.

The truth hit me hard. My eyes filled with water and tears rolled down my cheeks. I lay on the floor in a fetal position and blubbered like a baby. How had I lost my muse? We had a perfect relationship, once. I had always felt the most alive when my creativity and I were in sync. It was magic to feel her life force pumping through my veins, opening my heart, and aligning me to the cosmos. When we were together, everything was fun, silly, and playful. Together, we had unlimited possibilities.

But now something was off. I was vibrating at a different level from my creativity. Time was running out. How was I going to produce amazing, magical, powerful, magazine-worthy designs on my own?

As my tears dried and the reality of the situation set in, I accepted that my creativity was denying me entrance into her magical chamber. She'd abandoned me in my greatest time of need.

I smoothed down my orange T-shirt, rearranged my stones, and stood. I'd have to create the necklace alone.

And then it hit me. It takes two to tango. For as much as my creativity had abandoned me, so had I abandoned *her*.

I grabbed the hundreds of strands of crystals and placed them carefully into an open box. I made them a promise: From this moment forward, they would come with me wherever I went. If this relationship was going to work, we needed to spend more time together. We had to become each other's priority. Together, my beads and I attended dinner parties, went to the grocery store, sweated it out in yoga class, and slept together (you know, side by side).

As my deadline loomed closer, something finally started to break open between us. The more I interacted with the crystals, the more they interacted with me. I realized that I had forgotten how many layers there were to them, how different they looked depending on the light or environment. Instead of being angry with them, I started remembering why I had fallen in love with them in the first place.

And then one day, I heard, "Combine the Larimar crystals with Labradorite, and add some pearls." I jumped. *Did I just hear what I think I did?* Wary of questioning the voice further, I slipped my hand into the box and gently lifted out the beads. To my astonishment, I started creating patterns. Gorgeous, beautiful, magical patterns! Within 15 minutes, my first design was done. It was perfect—it felt energetically balanced and complete.

My heart sang. I promised my creativity that I would never take her for granted again. I made my deadline without a second to spare. The numerology collection was a huge success, and the necklace named Seven was featured in *Elle* magazine.

Perhaps you too have felt your creativity pull away. Maybe, like me, you've even felt abandoned by her. If so, then this chapter is for you.

LESSONS FROM THE CRYSTALS

By carrying around the box of beads, I solidified the connection between my creativity, my heart, and the crystals. We were in sync once again. I came to realize that I was the one who had locked her out. I had been so mentally focused on my deadline that I had temporarily suffocated her. I was no longer creating from my heart. The moment I stopped having fun with my creativity, I could no longer hear her. It wasn't that she left me, it was that I had shut her out.

I also learned that everything has its own time. Pushing harder to make things happen can sometimes take you farther from where you need to be. It was only when I changed my strategy and got out of my own way that I was able to open the path for my muse to return. Without the deadline, I might have quit designing the numerology series altogether and moved on to something else. In hindsight,

the deadline was my biggest blessing. It forced me to be uncomfortable and confront myself. I always had the choice to quit, but I knew that surge and euphoria of being in the creative flow, and I wanted it back. I wanted *me* back.

Creativity encourages the human spirit to look further into the possibilities that reside within. Crystals have the ability to do the same. Each one has its own story to tell. Within its walls are the messages and wisdom of the Earth. The way to tap into that wisdom is through silence. By breathing deeply and placing two crystals on your body with the intention of fully opening yourself to the energy of love, you'll be granted access into a magical place of creativity. In the silence, you can hear the inner voice of your heart. This voice knows you better than the voice in your mind.

The crystals taught me to reconnect not only with the energy and wisdom of the Earth, but to reconnect to my heart. The minute I did that, the floodgates opened.

TAPPING INTO YOUR
CREATIVE HEART RITUAL

TIME FRAME:
11 minutes daily for 7 consecutive days

Your heart always leads you in the right direction. How will you know? You will be filled with renewed passion, inspiration, and bliss. This ritual will reconnect you to your inner child, who likes to play, get messy, and feel the creative love.

WHAT YOU'LL NEED:

1 Carnelian heart for creativity, passion, and joy

1 Rose Quartz heart for opening the heart to unconditional love

1 journal

Your favorite pen

A timer

1 sage stick

1 feather

1 abalone shell or fireproof container to catch ashes from the sage

RITUAL STEPS:

1. Sage your environment, and cleanse your crystals (page 22).
2. Hold the crystals in your hands, close your eyes, and take 3 deep breaths. Aloud or in your head, say the following: *"I ask that the highest vibration of love and light connect with my highest self to clear all unwanted energy and any previous programming. I command these crystals to hold the intention of creativity, heart connection, and imagination. Thank you, thank you, thank you."*
3. When you go to bed, lie down, and place the Carnelian over your sacral chakra (your lower abdomen to navel area) and the Rose Quartz over your heart.
4. Keep the crystals on your body for a minimum of 6 minutes. The number 6 is the number of love and connects with the heart.
5. As you rest in stillness with your crystals, ask your heart to guide you to receive creative and inspirational messages. When you find the connection between your creativity and heart, that's where the magic happens.

6. After you've finished, place the crystals under your pillow, and allow the energies they hold to work as you sleep.

7. When you awaken in the morning, grab your crystals, journal, and pen, and find a comfortable spot with a flat surface where you can write in your journal.

8. Place the Rose Quartz heart next to your journal.

9. Hold the Carnelian heart in your non writing hand, and set the timer for 5 minutes.

10. Begin writing. Allow all the messages that were downloaded during the night to be put on paper. Even if some of the messages seem silly, don't discount them, as they may lead you to another creative idea.

11. Repeat steps 3 to 10 for 7 consecutive days.

Carnelian

COLOR: Reddish orange

ORIGIN: Found in many locations around the world, including Brazil, Madagascar, and India

HISTORY AND LORE: Carnelian is the life of the party. This crystal is all about vibrancy—from its color to its energy. If you feel trapped or bored within your mind space, Carnelian is the energy you will want to invite inside. The ancient Egyptians wore these blood-colored gems to add vitality and life to their otherwise lacking garments.

HEALING PROPERTIES: Creative juices seem to flow more easily with this crystal, known for empowering passion. Whether you need to boost your sex life, work life, or creative life, Carnelian will inject you with a surge of vitality. Use it when your self-esteem or confidence is being tested. This stone activates the sacral chakra for sex and creativity. It will encourage you to connect with your basic instincts. This is the perfect crystal for people who work in creative fields and need a punch of brave, motivational energy.

GET OUT OF YOUR COMFORT ZONE

Timmi and I have completely different creative processes. I have a hard time creating with too much structure, while she thrives on structure. I'm the yin to her yang (or maybe it's the other way around).

Timmi is a multitasker; her motto in life is, "Get it done." Just when you think she's checking e-mail or listening to an audio book, she'll jump into a conversation happening in the next room.

Timmi is also a list maker. When I finished the numerology collection and showed her the new necklaces, she was excited about the design but even more excited that I had made the deadline. (I always make it in the nick of time, but that stresses her out.)

Immediately Timmi started to make a list of more things to do. Without even looking up at me, she said, "There's so much to do now that the collection's finished. I want to make sure everything gets done." This was when *her* creative process began.

"It's my way of bringing creative structure and organization into my life," Timmi will say. Not surprisingly, I'm just the opposite. Writing too many lists hinders my process, and I lose my creative flow. The combination of our creative processes creates the perfect synergy, and the end result is better than we could ever achieve individually.

The ritual that follows will do for you what Timmi and I do for each other—get you out of your comfort zone so you can get out of your own way.

BUSTING OUT
OF THE BOX RITUAL

TIME FRAME:
However long it takes to get you out of your box!

It's normal to want to stay in your comfort zone. It's the perfect place for you to feel safe, content, and secure. But staying in that comfort zone really does put you in a box and smothers your creative potential. Boxes are small and restrictive; they prevent you from growing and expanding.

If you long for more creativity, ask yourself, *Am I living my life constrained in a box?* If the answer is *yes*, this is your wake-up call. It's time to mentally, physically, and emotionally leave your comfort zone behind so you can enter into a new space of creative brilliance. The act of physically cutting open a box reprograms your mind so that you can access the limitless possibilities of the universe.

WHAT YOU'LL NEED:

1 box—a shoe box, cereal box, or cracker box (any type of box will do)

1 pair of scissors

1 black marker

1 Clear Quartz point for growth, expansion, and unlimited creative potential

1 gold metallic pen that can be used to write on your crystal

1 sage stick

1 feather

1 abalone shell or fireproof container to catch ashes from the sage

RITUAL STEPS:

1. Sage your designated space, and cleanse your crystal (page 22).
2. Use your scissors to cut the box open until it's completely flat and you can see the whole interior.
3. Using the black marker, write all over the inside of your box with words, phrases, and pictures that represent your fears, regrets, limiting thoughts, or anything you feel holds you back from reaching your creative potential.

4. When you've written everything you want to include, tear up the box, and throw it away. By throwing away the box, you energetically release your self-imposed limitations and make space for the creativity you desire.

5. Hold the Clear Quartz point in your hands, close your eyes, and take 3 deep breaths. Aloud or in your head, say the following: *"I ask that the highest vibration of love and light connect with my highest self to clear all unwanted energy and any previous programming. I command this crystal to hold the intention of creativity, inspiration, and expansion. I release any limitations that surround me. Thank you, thank you, thank you."*

6. Using the gold metallic pen, write words on each side of the Clear Quartz point that represent what you wish to expand, create, or shift into. This programs your point to hold these energies for you as you make your shift.

7. Place your Clear Quartz point on a table next to your bed, and allow its energy to work with you as you sleep. Every morning when you wake up, you'll see it and be reminded to live your life expanding outside the box.

CREATING THROUGH THE EYES OF A CHILD

Every year, Timmi and I work with kids in the local community. We volunteer to teach art classes where we show the students how to make gemstone bracelets. Because children learn about earth science in elementary school, they're usually familiar with the mineral world. Many of them can identify the stones by color, mineral content, and even the region where they're found.

Every time we start a class, we ring a Tibetan singing bell. Often without being prompted, the kids will immediately sit in meditation position—legs crossed, hands on knees, palms up. (Well, it *is* California!)

We always bring in a large variety of beads and let the students choose whatever they want for their bracelets. There are no guidelines. When everyone's finished, we have them sit in a circle, where they will each stand and show off their creations. We encourage the children to give each other positive feedback. This process allows them to see that one idea (a bead bracelet) can be interpreted in many different ways. It also gives everyone a safe, judgment-free environment, allowing them the freedom to have fun and be creative.

These classes are some of our most rewarding events every year. They remind us of what it was like when we were kids, creating with no boundaries, simply guided by our hearts. We didn't care so much then about the end result or even what anybody else thought.

We've heard it said that "the creative adult is the child who survived." But sometimes even for the creative adult, the daily responsibilities of life force the creative spirit into hiding. As adults, we can simply fail to see the value of the inner child. We need to recapture that childlike sense of innocence and wonder. But how?

To get out of a creative slump, the best thing you can do is begin creating something— *anything*. Start with baby steps. Don't expect to go from 0 to 10 within hours; the process takes time!

The next ritual will inspire your inner child to come back and play. The Creative Spirit Stick you'll design in this ritual will be a visual representation of the playful creativity that lives within you. While you're collecting the treasures to decorate your stick, you'll have time for inner reflection. Each item will require you to decide if it resonates with who you are right now. Keep note—or, if you're like Timmi, make a list—of what attracts you for your stick. These items will represent a reinvented version of your creative self.

Always remember there's no wrong or right way to do this ritual. The most important part is to have fun, try something new, and listen to your heart. Then whenever your to-do list threatens to take up all your time, the Creative Spirit Stick will remind you to embrace your inner child again.

CREATIVE SPIRIT STICK RITUAL

TIME FRAME:
It's up to you. How long will you allow yourself to play?

You're about to embark on a creative treasure hunt to collect items to decorate your Creative Spirit Stick. The sky's the limit; the most important thing is to take your time and not rush the process. Make sure everything you choose has meaning. For one person, a seashell might represent coming out of their shell, while to someone else, it might represent gourmet dishes with shellfish. Maybe you received a gift with the perfect ribbon that you can wrap around your spirit stick.

Let yourself be playful, and let finding the materials be an adventure that gets your creative juices flowing again.

WHAT YOU'LL NEED:

1 wood stick that's roughly 12" long and at least 1" in diameter. The wood stick acts as a physical symbol of your creative self. The energy of wood is foundational, thus giving your creativity a solid foundation. If you don't live in an area where sticks are readily available, visit a local craft store. (You may need to remove the bark from your stick in order to allow your embellishments to adhere to it.)

6 stones that represent the colors of the rainbow—red, orange, yellow, green, blue, and purple. Tapping into these rainbow colors can awaken the childlike wonder within your soul.

• Red is for passion. Pick a red-toned crystal such as Red Jasper or Garnet to reclaim energy and action.

• Orange is for creativity. Pick an orange-toned crystal such as Carnelian or Sunstone to ignite enthusiasm and joy.

• Yellow is for happiness. Pick a yellow-toned crystal such as Pyrite or Yellow Jasper for light and opportunity.

• Green is for harmony. Pick a green-toned crystal such as Malachite or Aventurine for love and opening the heart.

• Blue is for communication. Pick a blue-toned crystal such as Sodalite or Lapis Lazuli for self-expression and truth.

• Purple is for intuition. Pick a purple-toned crystal such as Amethyst or Fluorite for spiritual growth and transformation.

1 glue gun and several glue sticks

1 pair of scissors

Any additional materials to make your stick feel as colorful, playful, and creative as you wish, such as yarn, additional crystals, bells, ribbon, raffia, thread, fabric, dried flowers, or seashells.

1 sage stick

1 feather

1 abalone shell or fireproof container to catch ashes from the sage

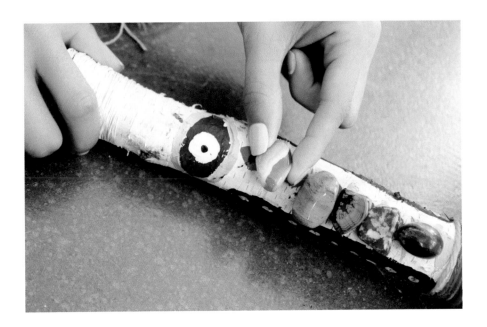

RITUAL STEPS:

1. Sage your environment, and cleanse your crystals (page 22).

2. Hold the 6 stones (and any others you added) in your hands, close your eyes, and take 3 deep breaths. Aloud or in your head, say the following: *"I ask that the highest vibration of love and light connect with my highest self to clear all unwanted energy and any previous programming. I command these crystals to hold the intention of connection, creativity, and inspiration. Thank you, thank you, thank you."*

3. We like to place the crystals in the order of the colors of the rainbow, and glue them starting at the bottom of the stick. If you'd like to follow this, start at the bottom, glue the red crystal, followed by the orange, yellow, green, blue, and purple crystals. Gluing the crystals in a row is just a suggestion, of course. You can glue them anywhere you want—there are no rules!

4. Decorate the stick with any remaining materials you like.

5. When you've completed your Creative Spirit Stick, connect with it by placing it in a space where you'll journal, paint, garden, work, and so on. Remember that your stick was made with your creative energy, and it holds that energy for you to tap into whenever you need it. Trust yourself! Your creative spirit is always within you, waiting for you.

Sunstone

WISDOM KEEPER:
SEDUCTRESS

COLOR: Mostly orange or red and can have hints of brown, gray, and white

ORIGIN: Canada, India, Norway, Russia, and the U.S.

HISTORY AND LORE: Just as the Sun brings life to all living things on Earth, Sunstone will breathe life into your creative spirit. Sunstone promotes energy, vitality, and creativity. A Native American legend says that Sunstone came from the blood of a great warrior who was wounded by an arrow. The warrior's blood, which gave Sunstone its shade of red, carried his spirit into the stone. In Viking culture, Sunstone acted as a compass. Sunstone was placed on a ship's mast to point voyages and spirits in the right direction.

HEALING PROPERTIES: The effervescent energy of Sunstone is inspiring. This stone nourishes the sacral chakra, encouraging confidence, power, and leadership. Freed from self-doubt, your creativity will flourish.

"Creativity for me is driven by nature. Each season reveals a new crop of ingredients or what can be deemed a fresh palette for me to create. Mother Nature is the inspiration in my kitchen."

— LUDO LEFEBVRE,
celebrity chef and television personality

CHAPTER 14

THE NOW OF SPIRITUALITY

EMBRACING THE LIGHT AND DARK
ON YOUR SPIRITUAL JOURNEY

*"The true concept of destiny is ultimately vibrating
and broadcasting the biggest, most compassionate
version of yourself."*

— GURU JAGAT,
*senior Kundalini Yoga teacher and founder
of RA MA Institute, TV, and Records*

LIFE ALWAYS COMES FULL CIRCLE. AS A LITTLE GIRL, I OFTEN SPENT MY SUMMERS ON THE ISLANDS OF HAWAII. IT ISN'T SURPRISING, then, that my journey with crystals began on the Big Island.

Over 20 years ago, I stumbled upon a book about crystals and chakras and was so inspired that I called the author and asked if she would meet with me. To my surprise, she said, "Yes!" I booked a ticket for Hawaii the next day, and my journey with the crystals officially began.

Once I arrived at her home, the scent of plumeria flowers filled the air. I was lulled by the palm trees swaying in the wind. She led me to a healing room and instructed me to lie down on a thick mat on the floor. One of the first things she told me was how important it was that I go visit Pele, the legendary volcano goddess whose home is in the craters of Kilauea. Since Pele holds the essence of the Big Island, she told me it was important that I physically experience her energy by walking on the volcano.

The more I learned about Pele, the more I became intrigued by her energy. Some people consider Pele to be a Hawaiian myth, but many believe she's real. She's a goddess of the Earth who destroys with her molten lava flames to make room for the creation of new life. Her presence is mesmerizing and unpredictable. She might be active and visible one day, but quiet the next.

After the author explained Pele's energy, she said, "I'm now going to lay crystals on and around your body so that you can feel Pele's healing energy of transformation, which can create a new beginning in your life." I remember this moment so clearly. Within seconds, I felt my body travel deeper and deeper into the core of the Earth. It felt as if I was rooted, grounded, and nurtured all at the same time, as if Mother Earth was cradling me in her arms.

After some time, the foundation underneath my body was uprooted, and a surge of energy went through my spine. I was now energetically above my body, no longer enclosed within my physical form. It was like I was floating in space on a giant crystal. I had transmuted into a streaming multidimensional beam of light expanding into the universe.

An hour passed. When I opened my eyes, I knew that a doorway had been opened for me to access another dimension—one that existed beyond time and space. I would never look at my life the same way again. An entire universe existed beyond what my physical eyes could see. Yet, at the same time, I knew this universe also resided within me; it was just a matter of accessing it.

For years I continued my studies of ancient healing modalities with various kahunas on the islands.

When we first began working on this book, Timmi and I decided to take another journey to Hawaii together. Years ago, at the beginning of our business, we had promised ourselves that we would do one thing every year to learn something new about the world of wellness and spirituality. For the book, we wanted to make sure we were on the cutting edge of the crystal world, so we traveled back to Hawaii to reconnect to the islands' magical energy.

Some say each of the seven Hawaiian Islands corresponds to one of the seven chakras in the body. Our initial plan was to visit three specific islands that would help us reconnect to a peaceful mind, a relaxed body, a warm heart, and the spirit of aloha. To reignite the flame within our physical bodies, we would go to the Big Island—the island of fire, transformation, and new life. It's linked with the first, or root, chakra, which is associated with security, survival, and everything solid in life (home, body, and the ground we walk on).

The second stop would be Molokai to reconnect to the spirit of love. This island is considered to be the heart of Hawaii and is linked to the fourth, or heart, chakra. The third and final stop would be Kauai, the oldest island, which is connected to insight and intuition. It's linked to the sixth, or third eye, chakra and is a place to clear and expand the mind.

We've often heard that the islands either embrace you or kick you out. If you respect them, tap into Mother Nature, and stay open to receiving their messages of synchronicity, you'll be guided on a life-changing, magical journey. We were about to find out if that theory was true.

FIRST STOP, THE BIG ISLAND: CONNECTING WITH THE BODY

From the moment we stepped foot on the Big Island, we felt the vital life force that permeated the land. It was alive! We heard a strong message that we'd be able to reconnect with our true nature as we tapped into the healing power of Mother Nature.

To reground and reconnect with our physical bodies, we decided to drive around the entire island, stopping at sacred sites along the way. The Big Island isn't called "big" for nothing, so we had long stretches of uninterrupted time between each stop to clear our minds and reclaim our inner stability. During this time, we allowed ourselves the space to rediscover what we each needed in order to let go, heal, and thrive.

As we drove farther and farther into the island, the scenery looked like another planet, morphing from lush greenery to large areas of uninhabited parcels of land, to barren lava, to forests full of tropical rainstorms. Then suddenly the Sun would burst through the clouds to reveal white sandy beaches.

I had an abrupt realization that how quickly these conditions changed was a metaphor for life. Traveling around the Big Island, it became crystal clear how easy it is to stay stuck in our thoughts, feelings, and emotions. The truth is, all we have is the moment of *now*. Whether we like it or not, we have to continually adapt to different climates and scenery.

At some point, we'd been driving for so long that my mind started to unwind, and a game of hide-and-seek began. In the silence of the drive, I came face-to-face with the part of myself who wanted to seek the truth of who I really was, as well as the part of me who wanted to hide from my shadow side.

The hours passed and the scenery continued to change. Questions started to fill my mind. *Why do I hold on to these limiting beliefs of shame, guilt, and worry? Why do I choose to stay hurt and harbor resentment against those in my past who I once considered good friends, work associates, and old lovers? How can this serve me in any way?*

Sure, every hurtful situation could easily be justified in my mind, but the other person had already moved on. Why hadn't I? By holding on to the resentment, I was the only one who was continuing to be hurt. And worst of all, those dark emotions were energetically stored in my physical body. Talk about an energy suck and emotional downer!

When we got out of the car to walk on the beautiful Big Island, the majesty of the Earth made me realize how insignificant those resentments were. *Now* was the time to let them go, and Hawaii offered the perfect practice for us—Ho'oponopono, which means "to make right."

I had already discovered this ancient practice of reconciliation and forgiveness when I visited Hawaii years earlier and was introduced to a Hawaiian medicine woman named Nahi Guzman. Ho'oponopono is a practice to clean up and correct any problems in your life. As we forgive others, we also forgive ourselves.

Nahi would do Ho'oponopono for me whenever I visited her in person. Back in California, she would work on Timmi or me via phone. Oftentimes she would clear the air between us or within our business.

When she passed away, I felt that a piece of Hawaii had left my heart. I never stopped missing Nahi, but I stopped doing Ho'oponopono. And because of that, I had forgotten how important it is to forgive ourselves and others in order to heal the physical energy of the body.

That day on the Big Island with Timmi, I remembered. We gathered our crystals, grounded into the land, and did Ho'oponopono. When we were finished, we felt lighter, happier, and limitless.

MAKE THINGS RIGHT RITUAL (HOʻOPONOPONO)

TIME FRAME:
11 minutes daily for 7 consecutive days

In today's fast-paced society, we are constantly bombarded by information. It has never been more important to remain grounded than it is right now.

When you're grounded, centered, balanced, and connected with the Earth's energy, it's easier to stay collected no matter what happens. A strong foundation is characteristic of a balanced first, or root, chakra which is the base of all your chakras and sets the groundwork for the other six.

In order to gain the benefits of Hoʻoponopono, it's important to be grounded into the energy of the Earth so that you feel supported. In its simplest form, Hoʻoponopono is a self-healing practice of taking full responsibility for everything in your life—good and bad—and working toward making it right. It's a continual process of personal development that focuses on four aspects: feeling sorry, forgiveness, thankfulness, and love.

This ritual will help you ground into the rooted energy of the first chakra and take full ownership of what isn't working in your life. By allowing yourself the time and space to forgive yourself and others, you reclaim your power and open the door to a new beginning.

WHAT YOU'LL NEED:

2 Black Onyx stones to release unwanted energies

2 Red Jasper stones for stability and nurturing

1 Smoky Quartz stone to ground and let go

1 Shungite stone to neutralize any energy that's released throughout the duration of the ritual

1 small abalone shell to bring calming and healing energy

1 sage stick

1 feather

1 abalone shell or fireproof container to catch ashes from the sage

RITUAL STEPS:

-----

1. Sage your environment, and cleanse your crystals (page 22).
2. Hold the crystals in your hands, close your eyes, and take 3 deep breaths. Aloud or in your head, say the following: *"I ask that the highest vibration of love and light connect with my highest self to clear all unwanted energy and any previous programming. I command these crystals to hold the intention of forgiveness, gratitude, and love. Thank you, thank you, thank you."*
3. Lie down in a comfortable position, flat on your back. You may need to have someone help you place the crystals on your body. Place the crystals in a downward-facing triangular-shaped grid over your pelvic area, where your first chakra is located. A triangle is a symbol that connects the mind, body, and spirit, and a downward-facing triangle represents the power of the divine feminine.
4. Place the 2 Black Onyx stones at the inside of each hipbone on your lower stomach, creating the two top corners of the triangle.
5. Place the Smoky Quartz stone in between the Black Onyx stones to finish the top edge of the triangle.
6. Place the Shungite stone on top of your pubic bone to form the lower point of the triangle.
7. Place the 2 Red Jasper stones between the Shungite and the Black Onyx to finish off the remaining two sides.
8. Place the small abalone shell in the center of the triangle.
9. Keep the crystals on your body for a minimum of 11 minutes, as you think about what you want to release and "make right" in your life.
10. Use words from the traditional Ho'oponopono practice. As you say:

    a. *"I'm sorry"*—you acknowledge whatever you've attracted into your life and take full responsibility for it.

    b. *"Please forgive me"*—you ask for forgiveness for anything you have knowingly or unknowingly done to others or to yourself.

    c. *"Thank you"*—you express thanks for the experiences that allowed you the opportunity to learn and grow.

    d. *"I love you"*—you give love to yourself and all that is. Love is the highest vibration that exists.

11. You may say these four verses in any order you wish and as many times as feels right to you. As your heart opens and heals, allow miracles to come your way!
12. Repeat steps 3 to 11 daily for 7 consecutive days.

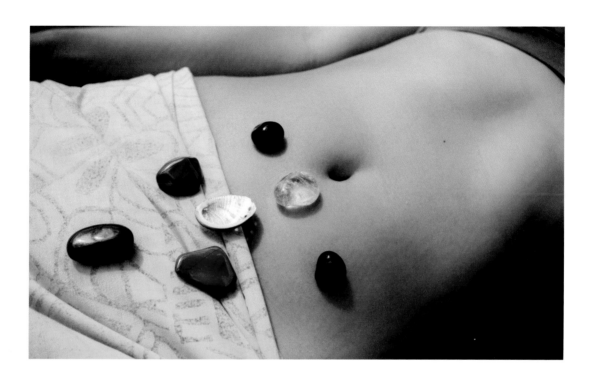

Red Jasper

THE STABILIZER

COLOR: Red

ORIGIN: Found in many places, including Brazil, India, Madagascar, Venezuela, and the U.S.

HISTORY AND LORE: Red Jasper is a mood stabilizer. Jasper comes in many shades. Red Jasper owes its blush to iron impurities. This blood hue convinced the Dutch that Red Jasper could control blood flow. Since the 1500s, this crystal has been used to aid in conception and creative fervor.

HEALING PROPERTIES: Red Jasper is associated with the root chakra. Activating your sacral chakra with Red Jasper is thought to increase sexual desire. This stone will also help to stabilize emotional turbulence. If you are a worrier, bring Red Jasper into your energy field. This will work to dim those constant, toxic thoughts.

The 7 Chakras

NAME	LOCATION	ENERGETIC CONNECTION	COLOR	CRYSTALS
1st Root Chakra	Base of spine or coccyx	Security Survival Everything solid in our lives (home, body, ground we walk on, etc.)	Red	Shungite Smoky Quartz Hematite Red Jasper Black Onyx
2nd Sacral Chakra	Lower abdomen	Sexuality Passion Creation Vulnerability Relationships	Orange	Carnelian Vanadinite Tangerine Quartz Orange Calcite Sunstone
3rd Solar Plexus Chakra	Upper abdomen	Personal Power Confidence Responsibility Willpower	Yellow	Citrine Yellow Jasper Pyrite Tiger's Eye
4th Heart Chakra	Heart	Love Forgiveness Connection with the mind, body, and spirit	Green and Pink	Ruby Zoisite Unakite Rose Quartz Rhodonite Chrysoprase Fuchsite Malachite
5th Throat Chakra	Throat	Self-knowledge Communication Speaking your truth	Blue	Turquoise Sodalite Blue Apatite
6th Third Eye Chakra	Forehead, between the eyes	Intuition Personal Wisdom Emotional Intelligence	Purple	Amethyst Fluorite Lapis Lazuli Indigo Gabbro
7th Crown Chakra	The very top of the head	Connection to our spiritual nature Higher consciousness	Violet and White	Lepidolite Amethyst Clear Quartz Lemurian Quartz

SECOND STOP, MOLOKAI: CONNECTING WITH THE HEART

Getting to Molokai became the most frustrating and time-consuming part of our trip. Our flight schedule proved to be a problem, and we had to change the date of our appointment with a healer we were to meet named Zelie. Luckily she was able to accommodate us, and it was well worth the effort.

When we landed on Molokai, it was as if we had just jumped through an invisible energetic shield of protection around it. Zelie smiled when we arrived and said, "So, you made it! I wasn't sure . . . a lot of people say they're coming, but never make it." We understood why!

We talked for several hours with this wise and soulful woman, but we could have chatted well into the night. "Molokai is the island of potent prayer. It was the most intense training ground for kahunas, or Hawaiian shamans," she told us. "It was where they learned that both light and dark sides of life exist."

She continued to explain that if we never acknowledge our shadow selves, we can't know ourselves fully. I understood what she was saying, even though as children, most of us were never taught to look at the shadow side of ourselves. It isn't something the average family talks about at the dinner table. "Hey, I'm afraid of being vulnerable, rejected, and abandoned. How about you?"

Zelie acknowledged that there are different layers on the spiritual path, and it takes spiritual maturity to deal with our shadows. When we start on a spiritual journey, most of us only want to acknowledge the light. When we do begin to look at the shadow, it can be difficult, especially if we're not grounded in the body and connected to our heart center. It's best to ease into shadow work.

While sitting with her and gazing at the ocean in the heart center of the Hawaiian Islands, both Timmi and I knew we needed to explore the shadow further.

Molokai taught us that to see ourselves in our entirety, we must work with both sides—the light and shadow, the good and the bad. They're never truly separate.

Most of us start our spiritual journey in a light-filled state, basking in the pure bliss of it all. As we mature on the path, however, we must make a crucial shift to acknowledge the aspects of ourselves that we don't want to see. We must embrace these darker shadows and concede that they are very much a part of who we are.

We went to Molokai looking at our spiritual journey from a purely mind-based perspective, but we left with the realization that we need to be more heart-centered. The heart is where we feel, connect with our truth, and make our dreams come true. By making space in our hearts for the shadow side, we acknowledge all aspects of ourselves and get to know the totality of who we are. When we embrace our shadows, we're completely transparent with ourselves; it's only then that we have the tools to reach our highest potential and truly live in the now.

OPENING YOUR HEART TO YOUR SHADOW RITUAL

TIME FRAME:
11 minutes daily for 7 consecutive days

Whether we're willing to admit it or not, we all have a shadow side. It consists of the aspects we've repressed and pushed way down deep into the unconscious. We do this because we believe that these parts of us are unacceptable.

Our life experiences shaped the way we feel and programmed us to repress "negative emotions," such as shame, sadness, fear, guilt, and anger. But in order to know who we are wholeheartedly, we need to make space in our hearts for these shadow aspects, acknowledging their existence and letting them surface so that the emotions can be released.

If you want, you can combine this ritual with the Make Things Right Ritual (page 243). You'll enter a grounded and centered state, and you'll open your heart to the darker aspects of yourself. When you know that light resides in these shadow selves, you'll be less likely to repress them and more likely to become who you really are.

WHAT YOU'LL NEED:

2 Rhodonite stones for forgiveness, compassion, and releasing fear

1 small Shungite stone for neutralizing any energy that's released during the duration of the ritual

1 Ruby Zoisite stone for transmuting negative energy into positive

1 Rose Quartz heart for opening the heart to unconditional love

1 small Selenite wand for light energy (it should fit comfortably in your hand)

1 Black Tourmaline crystal for clearing and releasing energy (it should fit comfortably in your hand)

1 sage stick

1 feather

1 abalone shell or fireproof container to catch ashes from the sage

RITUAL STEPS:

1. Sage your environment, and cleanse your crystals (page 22).

2. Hold the crystals in your hands, close your eyes, and take 3 deep breaths. Aloud or in your head, say the following: *"I ask that the highest vibration of love and light connect with my highest self to clear all unwanted energy and any previous programming. I command these crystals to hold the intention of letting go, allowing, and healing. Thank you, thank you, thank you."*

3. Lie down in a comfortable position, flat on your back. You may need to have someone help you place the crystals on your body.

4. You will be placing the crystals in an upward-facing triangular-shaped grid over your fourth, or heart, chakra. The triangle is a symbol that connects the body, mind, and spirit.

5. Place the 2 Rhodonite stones under each of your breasts or pectoral muscles. They will create the bottom two corners of the triangle.

6. Place the Shungite in between the Rhodonite stones.

7. Place the Rose Quartz heart over your heart.

8. Place the Ruby Zoisite 1" above the Rose Quartz heart to form the upper point of the triangle.

9. To bring in light energy, place the Selenite wand in your left, receiving hand.

10. Place the Black Tourmaline in your right hand to energetically release the dark shadow energies that no longer serve you.

11. Keep the crystals on your body for a minimum of 11 minutes as you visualize your light and shadow aspects coexisting within you. Allow your heart to open and accept the shadow side of you.

12. Now that you have acknowledged and accepted these shadow aspects, visualize the Selenite surrounding them with light, and release any negativity from the shadow into the Black Tourmaline stone.

13. Repeat steps 3 to 12 daily for 7 consecutive days. You're on the way to becoming your true self!

Rhodonite

—

COLOR: Pink with black veins

ORIGIN: Found in many locations, including Australia, Brazil, India, Madagascar, Mexico, Russia, Sweden, and the U.S.

HISTORY AND LORE: Rhodonite derives its name from the Greek word meaning "rose." Think of this crystal as your ally. Black and white manganese come together to form this vivacious red love stone. It is associated with love because it is believed to carry the properties of forgiveness. Russian czars would present Rhodonite as wedding gifts at royal weddings.

HEALING PROPERTIES: Forgiveness isn't easy. Rhodonite can help eliminate feelings of regret, sadness, and self-doubt. This stone will also inspire you to revive your self-worth and emotional balance. In connecting with the heart chakra, Rhodonite nourishes us with love from within. For it is only when we forgive ourselves and begin to love again that our spirit can rediscover passion.

THIRD STOP, KAUAI: CONNECTING WITH THE MIND

As soon as we landed on Kauai, we met a good friend, Shirin Hunt, who is a Theta-Healer. "Kauai is a powerful place," she said. "If you're open to the energy, it will take you for a ride. All your 'stuff' will be brought to the surface and mirrored back to you." This proved to be true.

Kauai had an extraordinarily synchronistic energy. Our thoughts and words seemed to manifest into reality within a much shorter time frame than we were used to. In fact, everything aligned at a faster pace. It was as if the island was a powerful teacher, showing us how much our reality is based on what we focus on mentally. Kauai's third eye chakra energy was exactly what we needed to expand our minds!

We decided to hike to Hanakāpī'ai Falls along the Nāpali Coast. It's an eight-mile hike up and back through lush jungle, and then 800 feet up vertically to the 300-foot cascading falls. Many have said it's one of the most beautiful waterfalls in the world.

Before we started the hike, it was important to determine if the weather conditions would work for us. We would have to cross three to four streams each way, and there's always the chance of flash flooding. Luckily no rainstorms were forecasted for the day, so we decided to move forward.

The first part of the hike was a brutal incline, but the majestic coastal scenery encouraged us to keep going. The scent of guavas filled the air, and a bamboo forest revealed itself to us. We felt an overwhelming connection with

Mother Nature while we took in her intoxicating oxygen. It was as if she was saying, "Keep going—look what's up ahead."

The next part of the hike brought us to a point of awe, self-doubt, and mental endurance. Mosquitoes were everywhere. Mud filled the trails. The rocky terrain was getting harder to navigate. And our minds began playing tricks on us. While our hearts wanted to move forward, our minds told us that our bodies were too tired and we had too far to go. Fearful thoughts ran through our heads: *Do we have enough water? How are we going to get over those huge slippery rocks? Maybe we should turn around now that the muddy red dirt is getting thicker.*

Just when we were about to turn back, a hiker appeared. "The falls are up ahead—you're almost there!" It was a sign from the universe that we needed to push on.

Three *more* hours passed. And still we hadn't reached the falls. The battle between our hearts and minds continued. Each time we decided to turn around, another hiker would appear, delivering the same message: "The falls are up ahead! You're almost there!"

At this point, we were discouraged and exhausted. We didn't know if we could go on. There was only one thing to do: We had to conquer our minds. We had to drown out the fear and focus on the love. Finally our hearts prevailed and we made it to the falls. We jumped into the cool, crisp water and swam to the swimming hole that led under the falling water. Mud and sweat washed off of us, but so too did our self-doubt, mental blocks, and limited thinking.

After a while, we got out of the water to sit inside a little alcove cave behind the falls. There, we were acutely aware that the human spirit longs for something more than a mind filled with endless chatter. While it may seem impossible to clear our minds of all thoughts, we can choose to fill the majority of our minds with what we want to create, such as joy and happiness.

Kauai asked us to look in the mirror, and what we saw were two people who had managed to conquer their minds and expand on their self-imposed limitations. We proved to ourselves that anything is possible. This ritual will help you do the same.

EXPANDING INTO THE MIND RITUAL

TIME FRAME:
11 minutes daily for 7 consecutive days

Now that you've connected your body with your heart, you'll need to expand your mind, uniting all three. If you place an upward-facing triangle on top of a downward-facing triangle, like in the crystal grids used in the Make Things Right (page 243) and Opening Your Heart to Your Shadow (page 249) rituals earlier in the chapter, you will create a symbol that resembles a six-pointed star or a one-dimensional *merkaba*.

The word *merkaba* originated as three separate words in ancient Egyptian: *mer*, meaning light—a light that rotates within itself; *ka*, meaning the human spirit; and *ba*, meaning the human body. The merkaba is a three-dimensional, sacred geometric shape that's considered a useful tool when trying to expand the possibilities of the mind, body, and spirit, guided by the heart. The energy of the merkaba is magnified when it's in the form of Clear Quartz crystal.

Lemurian Quartz crystal is one of the "master crystals," which are believed to be record keepers of the ancient civilization of Lemuria. Legend has it that Lemurian crystals were placed or seeded in various locations around the world to be found by those who were open and ready to work with their stored information. Many consider Hawaii to be where historic Lemuria existed. These crystals carry a high vibrational energy of light and hope, and help to activate and align your chakras. The grooves or ladderlike striations on Lemurian crystals are said to act as a "stairway to heaven."

By working with a Clear Quartz merkaba and Lemurian Quartz crystals, this ritual will allow for the seeding and growth of new ideas. It will help you believe you're capable of expanding beyond your current beliefs and abilities. Anything you desire is indeed possible!

WHAT YOU'LL NEED:

1 small Clear Quartz merkaba crystal for expansion and limitless possibilities

4 Lemurian Quartz crystals for planting the seeds of growth and new ideas

1 sage stick

1 feather

1 abalone shell or fireproof container to catch ashes from the sage

RITUAL STEPS:

If you want, you can combine the crystal rituals Make Things Right (page 243) and Opening Your Heart to Your Shadow (page 249) with this one to create a full crystal-body layout.

1. Sage your environment, and cleanse your crystals (page 22).

2. Hold the crystals in your hands, close your eyes, and take 3 deep breaths. Aloud or in your head, say the following: *"I ask that the highest vibration of love and light connect with my highest self to clear all unwanted energy and any previous programming. I command these crystals to hold the intention of intuition, expansion, and determination. Thank you, thank you, thank you."*

3. Lie down in a comfortable position, flat on your back. You may need to have someone help you place the crystals on your body.

4. Place one Lemurian crystal on the ground above your head with its point directed downward toward your head.

5. Place one Lemurian in each hand with the point facing in toward your body. Place the last Lemurian crystal between your ankles with the point facing upward toward your body.

6. Visualize that your mind, body, and heart center are being seeded with new ideas, blessings, and positive energy.

7. Place the Clear Quartz merkaba over your third eye, located slightly above the space between your eyes.

8. Keep the crystals on and around your body for a minimum of 11 minutes, and allow their loving and expansive energies to radiate throughout your body, heart center, and mind. Remember that your life is made up of endless possibilities.

9. Repeat steps 3 to 8 daily for 7 consecutive days.

"Spirituality invites us to step into the illuminated space directly behind your eyes, letting go of human interpretation and everything we think we know, so as to embrace Divine perception which is infinite and limitless. It is a call to trust that which we can't see, but 'know' to the depths of our very being—that the love that is within is the Source that calls us home and to the very God that is within in ALL."

— SEANE CORN,
yoga teacher, co-founder Off the Mat Into the World

Lemurian Quartz

—

WISDOM KEEPER:

TIME TRAVELER

COLOR: Clear to pale pink

ORIGIN: Brazil

HISTORY AND LORE: The ladderlike striations that ascend the facets of the Lemurian Quartz points offer an unusual variety of Quartz crystal. These stones are said to be left over from a lost Lemurian civilization. Their striations are thought to be programmed by a code that, if unlocked, could bring us into a new reality.

HEALING PROPERTIES: These wisdom keepers are the masters of love. Lemurian Quartz crystals work with all your chakras to cleanse and harmonize their balance of energy. The high vibrational capacity of Lemurian Quartz crystals will dissolve all energy blocks. Use this crystal in meditation by gently rubbing your thumb along the striations. This will help you achieve a better understanding of yourself and your spirituality.

THE END OF THE ROAD

———

As we traveled through the Hawaiian Islands in pursuit of new ways to share how to ground energy, heal hearts, and expand minds, we ended up healing ourselves.

Throughout the entire time that Timmi and I were in Hawaii, it felt as if we were driving to the end of the road. We kept seeing signs that read "End of the Road." At first we wondered if this was a sign that something was about to end. But after further contemplation, we realized it was something completely different: We were willing to go to the end of the road to find the information that will inspire others.

We're here to the end of the road to help *you*.

The spiritual path might be long and arduous, but you'll never be traveling it alone. Mother Earth has given you many tools to help guide you. We hope we have given you a better understanding of one of her most powerful tools, her wisdom keepers—the magical and ancient energy of crystals.

AFTERWORD

It's our hope that as a society, we'll begin to work with Mother Earth rather than against her. For millions of years, she has been evolving and adapting, ebbing and flowing. Her story lies deep within the crystals we have shown you in this book. Listen to them. Treat them with love, and they'll do the same for you. Crystals aren't just rocks; they're the wisdom keepers we've been waiting for to remind us that we're all a part of something bigger than ourselves. Once we remember this, there's nothing we can't do together.

GLOSSARY

ABALONE SHELL—known as the Ears of the Sea because of its intimate connection with the ocean. This shell is often used when smudging to snuff out burning sage.

AMETHYST—a natural stress reliever that also encourages inner strength, peace, spiritual growth, and intuition. It attracts positive energy while clearing out any negative energy.

ANGELITE—connects you with your angels to protect your entire body. It helps to relieve tension, stress, and anger while facilitating forgiveness and stimulating healing.

APOPHYLLITE—a high vibrational crystal that emanates light to spiritually energize your soul. Holding it helps to immediately reduce stress, fear, anxiety, and worry.

AURA—an invisible electromagnetic field of energy that extends anywhere from three to five feet from the body.

AVENTURINE—one of the luckiest crystals, especially for manifesting prosperity and wealth. Its lucky energy is said to boost your chances or odds in any situation.

BASALT—a dark, volcanic rock caused by the rapid cooling of basaltic lava. It brings stability, promotes courage, and raises your energy levels.

BLACK KYANITE—a balancing crystal that's beneficial for space clearing, energetic protection, and letting go of things that are no longer aligned with your highest good. It helps you align all your chakras, removing any imbalances or blocks within each center.

BLACK OBSIDIAN—holds a spiritually grounding vibration that connects you with the energy of the Earth. It also provides psychic protection and clears any negative energy from your aura.

BLACK ONYX—a powerful, protective crystal that helps to shield your mind, body, and spirit from negative energy. This stone protects your personal energy field and helps to calm your fears, leaving you feeling more secure and safe.

BLACK TOURMALINE—one of the most powerful crystals for protection and the elimination of negative energy. It helps to absorb electromagnetic energy and unlocks any energy blockages within your body or space.

BLOODSTONE—removes any energy blockages and negative energy from your body and aura. It increases endurance, promotes stamina, and brings energy.

BLUE APATITE—a motivational and inspirational crystal that clears your mind, strengthens your personal power, and stimulates creativity. Many use this crystal to assist with their weight-loss goals as well.

BLUE LACE AGATE—one of the best crystals for anxiety and stress relief. Its calming blue color emits soothing vibrations that bring peace of mind and relaxation.

CARNELIAN—a crystal of courage, vitality, sexuality, confidence, and action. It activates the first three chakras to bring a surge of life force and creative energies.

CELESTITE—known for inviting angels into your space and fostering your connection with the higher realms. It holds a gentle, uplifting energy that relieves heavy moods, sadness, and anxiety.

CHAKRA—a Sanskrit term for wheel. It is believed that there are seven main chakras or spinning wheels of energy that reside in the center of the body, starting with the first chakra at the base of the spine and continuing up the body to the seventh chakra at the top of the head. (See page 246 for additional information on each chakra and the crystals associated with each chakra center.)

CHRYSOCOLLA—a peaceful, soothing crystal that brings comfort in times of stress, change, and transition. It promotes clear communication and self-expression, and it increases your capacity to love.

CHRYSOPRASE—encourages joy, optimism, and happiness, activating and opening your heart chakra. It reminds you to allow yourself to receive with an open heart.

DUMORTIERITE—referred to as the stone of patience, opening the doors of insight and activating the third eye chakra. It enhances your willpower in regard to learning.

CITRINE—a gemstone of light, happiness, abundance, and manifestation. It's one of the few crystals that doesn't hold negative energy.

FLAME AURA QUARTZ—also called Titanium Quartz or Rainbow Quartz; a crystal that clears energy blocks, fear, and doubt, especially those impeding creativity. Connecting with its rainbow energy is said to shed light on your spiritual purpose in this lifetime.

CLEAR QUARTZ—a stone of clarity that activates and amplifies your programmed intention. It also raises the energy level of any other crystals it comes into contact with.

FLUORITE—a crystal that houses rainbows. It helps to restore balance and bring order to chaos. Fluorite also heightens your focus and brings clarity of mind.

CORDING—the sharing of energy that can act as a life force energy that connects two people. It can be positive or negative, as well as something that was intentional or occurred without your knowledge.

FRANKINCENSE—a high-vibrational, sacred resin harvested from the Somali coast and Arabian Peninsula. Burning it works to "disinfect" a space of negative energy while providing protection and elevating your spiritual awareness.

CRYSTAL GRID—a powerful tool for manifesting goals, desires, and intentions that unites the energies of the crystals, a sacred geometric pattern, and your intention. The combination of these three things helps to manifest results much faster.

FUCHSITE—often called the fairy crystal, as it leaves green and gold sparkling flecks, like fairy dust. It encourages joyfulness, relaxation, and miracles, connecting you with your heart on a deeper level.

GARNET—a stone of passion and energy that ensures the smooth flow of energy throughout the body. It connects with your root chakra to help you feel more grounded and connected to yourself in the present moment.

JADE—a stone of wealth, prosperity, and abundance that helps you attain your goals, see past self-imposed limitations, and manifest your dreams into reality.

GOLDSTONE—an energy generator that helps you achieve your goals. Its flecks of copper deflect any unwanted energies.

JASPER—said to symbolize the blood of the Earth. It connects you deeply with the vibrations of the Earth, bringing grounding energy and a deeper understanding of the power of nature.

GREEN CALCITE—radiates soothing and calming energies to restore balance to the mind, body, and spirit. It helps to dissolve old energy patterns and belief systems to bring in money and prosperity.

KAMBABA JASPER—provides you with the inspiration and courage to confront your fears head-on. It also alleviates stress and restores balance to your mind, body, and spirit.

HEMATITE—the ultimate grounding stone that leaves you feeling more balanced, calm, and centered. It eliminates any negativity from your body, drawing it from you into itself.

KUNZITE—a heart-based crystal that fills your life with the energy of love. It's also a beneficial crystal for relieving anxiety, stress, and even sleep issues like insomnia.

HIMALAYAN SALT—a powerful cleansing, purifying, and detoxifying energy tool for your home. It is said to absorb any negative energy, toxin, or allergen in your space, leaving behind a cleansed space full of light and positivity.

LABRADORITE—a crystal of destiny, awareness, and power that connects you with the energy of light. It creates an energetic shield that protects your aura and strengthens your personal energy supply.

INDIGO GABBRO—a magical, intuitive, and spiritual stone that's wonderful for meditation and connecting to the spiritual realm. Its energy grabs you and pulls your energy down toward the Earth's core, helping you to feel focused so that you can overcome distractions.

LAPIS LAZULI—a crystal of awareness, insight, and truth. It is one of the oldest gemstones, one that has existed in ancient tales since the beginning of time. The famous golden sarcophagus of King Tut was heavily decorated with Lapis Lazuli stones.

LEMURIAN QUARTZ—considered one of the "master crystals," teaching oneness and helping you to embrace your own individuality. The crystal's grooves or ladderlike striations are said to act as a "stairway to heaven," unlocking hidden messages and information stored within the crystal.

LEPIDOLITE—fosters tranquil, peaceful, and calming energy. It's one of the best crystals for relieving anxiety because it naturally contains lithium. Connect with this stone in times of stress and chaos.

LITHIUM QUARTZ—promotes emotional peace, stress relief, and relaxation. It's a powerful yet gentle stone that uplifts your mind, body, and spirit. It gets its pink color from the natural presence of lithium, which is often used in antidepressant and antianxiety medications.

MALA NECKLACE—often called "meditation garlands." Made with 108 beads, mala necklaces are traditionally used for Japa meditation, in which you say a mantra or affirmation repeatedly, using the beads to keep count.

MALACHITE—a stone of transformation that works to clear and cleanse the heart chakra. It helps to balance the mind to relieve scattered and unfocused feelings.

MANTRAS—an instrument of the mind for meditation or manifestation. Mantras are powerful sounds or vibrations that you can use to focus the mind and enter a deep state of meditation.

MOOKAITE—brings strong healing, grounding, and protective energies. Found in a range of vibrant, earthy colors, this stone encourages your sense of adventure and pushes you out of your comfort zone.

MOONSTONE—the stone of destiny. Strongly connected with the energy of the Moon, it balances the yin or feminine energy within the body. It's also one of the best crystals for fertility.

MOSS AGATE—connected with nature and the spirit of the Earth. It brings new beginnings and promotes the release of old habits, as it also attracts wealth and abundance.

NUUMMITE—one of the oldest minerals on Earth, formed over three billion years ago. It draws out negative or outside energies to purify your energy field, bringing stability and grounding energies to help you sleep.

OCEAN JASPER—the ideal crystal for lifting your spirits. It allows you to find happiness in the present moment, calming the mind, body, and spirit to create a constant state of bliss.

ORANGE CALCITE—an energizing stone that helps to get positive energy moving throughout the body, especially in areas of creativity and sexuality. It's a wonderful stone to carry whenever you're embarking on a new journey or endeavor.

PALO SANTO—a sacred wood that comes from the Palo Santo trees of South America. When it's burned, the smoke is said to have medicinal, cleansing, and therapeutic healing power that inspires creativity and brings blessings.

PEACOCK ORE—resembles the vibrant colors of a peacock's tail. It's a stone of creativity, happiness, innovation, and blessings that increases creative energies and stimulates new ideas.

PETRIFIED WOOD—was once a living, breathing tree that became fossilized over thousands of years. It calms your nerves and fears, filling you with feelings of well-being and security.

PHANTOM QUARTZ—occurs when the growth of the crystal is interrupted. Then the crystal begins to grow again. Each mineral deposit appears like a "ghost," or another crystal within the crystal, showing the life story and evolution of the crystal.

PROGRAMMING— imprinting your crystal with your focused intention.

PYRITE—invites in success, prosperity, and wealth. Its reflective surface deflects negative energy to act as a shield of protection.

RAINBOW OBSIDIAN— nurtures and rejuvenates the heart after the experience of an emotional trauma, such as a broken heart, mourning the loss of a loved one, or a period of grief. It helps to heal the heart and rejuvenate the emotional body.

RED JASPER—a powerful gemstone of protection and stability. It inspires a positive attitude, increasing your motivation and energy level to encourage you to take action in your life.

RHODONITE—a stone of forgiveness and compassion. Referred to as the rescue stone, it carries a powerful healing vibration that releases fear and can help with relationship problems.

ROSE QUARTZ—opens the heart to all types of love: love for yourself, love for your family, romantic love, and love of everything on Earth. It helps to raise your self-esteem, restore confidence, and balance the emotions.

RUBY ZOISITE—a combination of fiery Ruby and earthy Zoisite. Holding the energy of passion and patience, it's a stone of the heart that balances the male and female energies within the body.

SAGE—an herb with energy that's fundamental to clearing and cleansing negative energy from a person, space, or crystal. When burned or used to smudge, it's the quickest way to clear out negativity.

SELENITE—ideal crystal for energy cleansing. It's one of the few crystals that has the ability to quickly unblock stagnant energy and remove negative energy. It also evokes calming energy to bring deep peace and mental clarity.

SHUNGITE—the "miracle molecule" of the 21st century. Said to be around two billion years old, it detoxifies the body by absorbing and eliminating any negative or health hazardous energies. It's wonderful for EMF (electromagnectic field) protection, purification of the body, and overall healing and balance.

SMOKY QUARTZ—a grounding and stabilizing stone that brings centering energies. It helps to overcome negative emotions such as stress, fear, jealousy, and anger.

SMUDGING—the fastest and most effective way to cleanse and clear your space and crystals. Burning sage removes negative energy, neutralizes the energy of your space, and enhances your intuition. This act helps to relieve worries, open the mind, clear away negative thoughts and feelings, and harmonize the body by releasing the stress of your spirit.

SODALITE—due to its high salt, manganese, and calcium content, this stone has a harmonizing and soothing effect on the body. It helps to strengthen your confidence, communication, inspiration, and intuition.

SUNSTONE—carries the light and happy energies of the Sun. It's a very protective stone that stimulates your personal power, creativity, strength, and leadership qualities.

TANGERINE QUARTZ—connected with the sacral chakra, this crystal promotes creativity, emotional balance, and sensuality. It reminds you to keep a healthy balance between the giving and receiving aspects of your relationships with friends, family, and your partner.

TECTONIC QUARTZ—Clear Quartz crystals that are millions of years old. The striations and grooves on these crystals were created from movement in the tectonic plates deep within the Earth.

TURQUOISE—known as the master healer, it's said to be the bridge between heaven, sky, and the Earth. As a throat chakra stone, it fosters honest and open communication from the heart.

TIGER'S EYE—a solar stone of courage, strength, will, and personal power. It helps you to see the positive in any situation and increases feelings of optimism. It's also wonderful for bringing new opportunities, prosperity, and wealth.

UNAKITE—balances the heart chakra and the male and female energies that lie within everyone. It's a powerful stone for emotional healing, allowing us to address the negative emotions we're holding on to and transform ourselves from a place of love.

TOURMALINATED QUARTZ— a combination of Clear Quartz with inclusions of Black Tourmaline. It deflects negative energy while helping to unlock any energy blockages within the body.

VANADINITE—strongly associated with the element of fire and the sacral chakra, this crystal is a strong creativity and energy booster. It helps you to become more focused on your tasks, clearing any blocks—especially those impeding creativity.

TREE AGATE—connects you on a deeper level with the Earth and nature. It clears blockages within your body's energy field to open the flow of abundance and prosperity.

ZEBRA JASPER—unites the yin and yang energies. The white and black coloring represents balance. It allows us to see the good in a "bad situation," and recognize the "bad" in a good situation, to realize the truth of any situation.

RESOURCES

FOR CRYSTALS:

Energy Muse—www.energymuse.com

Local metaphysical shops and gem shows

**FOR ENERGY
CLEARING SUPPLIES:**

Floracopeia—www.floracopeia.com

Shamans Market—www.shamansmarket.com

Mountain Rose Herbs—www.mountainroseherbs.com

FOR SPIRITUAL INSPIRATION:

mindbodygreen—www.mindbodygreen.com

The Chalkboard Mag—thechalkboardmag.com

The Numinous—the-numinous.com

Tony Robbins—www.tonyrobbins.com

FOR MEDITATION PILLOWS:

Samaya—samaya.life

chattra—chattra.com

**MEDITATION STUDIOS
AND MINDFUL RETREATS:**

The Den (Los Angeles)—denmeditation.com

RA MA Institute—www.ramayogainstitute.com

MNDFL (New York)—www.mndflmeditation.com

Maha Rose Center for Healing—www.maharose.com

The Class by Taryn Toomey—taryntoomey.com

Ashley Neese—ashleyneese.com

INSCAPE (New York)—inscape.life

INDEX

Ownership Ritual, *85–86*
as process, 76
Prosperity Necklaces and,
76–77, 78, 95
spiritual wealth and, 79,
81–82
Spiritual Wealth Bowl
Ritual, *81–82*
Suze Orman on, 96
tips to boost, 78
Tony Robbins on, 75
Psychic Protection Power
Banding Ritual, *195–197*
Pyramids, about, 12
Pyrite
history and lore, 197
prosperity and, 78
qualities and healing
properties, **8**, **197**, **268**
rituals using, *78*, *81–82*,
89–93, *96–97*, *192–193*,
195–197, *233–237*

Q

Quartz. *See* Amethyst; Citrine;
Clear Quartz; Flame
Aura Quartz; Lemurian
Quartz; Lithium Quartz;
Phantom Quartz; Rose
Quartz; Rutilated
Quartz; Smoky Quartz;
Tangerine Quartz;
Tectonic Quartz;
Tourmalinated Quartz
Quotations
Ashley Neese, 197
Brené Brown, 141
Dayle Breault, 181
Denise Linn, 21
Edgar Cayce, 179
Guru Jagat, 239
Gustaf Strömberg, 18
J.K. Rowling, 99

Kartar Diamond, 34
Katy Perry, 115
Kelly Leveque, 165
Lady Gaga, 79
Lena Dunham, 7
Light Watkins, 56
Ludo Lefebvre, 237
Ruby Warrington, 221
Russell Simmons, 37
Seane Corn, 257
Shaman Durek, 59
Sophie Jaffe, 162
Susan Miller, 219
Suze Orman, 96
Tony Robbins, 75
Wayne Dyer, 113

R

Rainbow Obsidian, 141,
151–153, 166, 167, **268**
Recovery ritual, *173–174*
Red Jasper
history and lore, 245
qualities and healing
properties, **8**, **245**, **268**
rituals using, *133–137*,
233–237, *243–245*
Releasing Pain, Balancing
Emotions, and Recovery
Ritual, *173–175*
Resources, 271
Rhodochrosite, **8**
Rhodonite
conceiving and, 149
history and lore, 252
qualities and healing
properties, **8**, **252**, **268**
rituals using, *123*, *138–140*,
249–251
Rhyolite, **8**
Rituals
aligning with moon phases,
18

duration of, 17–18
faith, religion and, 17
intention and, 15–16, 17
multiple at same time, 17
programming crystals and,
16–17
shifting consciousness for, 17
staying disciplined during,
18
timing importance, 17–18
why they are effective, 17
Robbins, Tony, 75
Rose Quartz
conceiving, birth and, 149,
156
history and lore, 51, 137
Katy Perry on, 115
love and, 116, 128
qualities and healing
properties, **8**, **137**, **268**
rituals using, *78*, *123*,
133–137, *155*, *157–158*,
225–227, *249–251*
for sleep, 166
Rowling, J.K., 99
Ruby Zoisite, *249–251*, **269**
Rutilated Quartz, **8**

S

Sage, *23–24*, **269**
Sea salt/Himalayan salt, clearing
space with, *28*, 34
Selenite
history and lore, 29
qualities and healing
properties, **8**, **29**, **269**
rituals using, *31–37*, *42–44*,
157–158, *177–179*,
217–219, *249–251*
for sleep, 166
Self-reflection, 59–73. *See also*
Meditation

ACKNOWLEDGMENTS

*You're writing a book about us? It must
be because of our magnetic personalities!*

muse /myōōz/ *noun.* a guiding spirit or source of inspiration

The Ultimate Muses:
Mother Earth and her Crystals

Muse of Vision: Patty Gift

Muse of Guidance: Wendy Sherman

Muse of Wisdom and Words:
Jennifer Gooch Hummer

Muse Who Puts Up with the Muses:
Sara Carter

Behind-the-Scenes Muses:
The Energy Muse Team

Muses of Unconditional Love and Patience: Jason, Orion, Sofia Rose, Jim, JB, Will, and our four-legged, furry friends

Muses of Support: Dee and Dan, Danny, Tim and Terry, Nana, and all of our family and friends

Muses on the Other Side: Grandma Meyer, Grandma Natalia, Nanu, Grandma Jo, Gustav Schindler, Michael Crisp, Nahi Guzman, Kalua Kaiahua, Cecilia Garcia, and Marlana Moench

Muses of Guidance: Bobby Lake-Thom, Grand Master Yap, Master Sang, Melody, and all of our teachers, mentors, and guides along our crystal journey

Tribe of Muses: Sally Lyndley, Jessica Carreiro, Lori Bregman, Betsy McLaughlin, Michelle Craig, Erica Kmiec, Ligia Allaire, Jocelyn Delaney, Melanie Votaw, Lena Dunham, Kartar Diamond, Shirin Hunt, Zelie Duvauchelle, Kahuna Ed, Dayle Breault, Light Watkins, Shaman Durek, Sophie Jaffe, Kelly LeVeque, Ashley Neese, Ruby Warrington, Ludo Lefebvre, Guru Jagat, Seane Corn, Ian Freshman, Kathy Lombard, Tatyana Tokina, David Cho, Elise Asch, Alberto Amuro, Lynn Creighton, Rena Joy, Christiane Northrup, Jason Wachob, Ruby Warrington, Jordan Younger, Jason Mraz, Jill Willard, Jody Gerson, Emma Mildon, Alexa Gray, Michael Gray, Claire Block, Sarah Hammond, Robert Goodman, John Grispon, Kevin McKinney, Gabrielle Bernstein, Molly Sims, Mary Alice Haney, Lisa Cheng, and the Energy Muse community

----

To all the muses who were honest with us, who advised us, who inspired us and who believed in us when no one else did. We would not have stayed on this journey without you. Your love and support never goes unnoticed.

ABOUT THE AUTHORS

Having known one another since the age of six, Energy Muse co-founders **Heather Askinosie** and **Timmi Jandro** are each other's yin to their yang. Heather is a leading influencer on the power of crystals, Feng Shui, and holistic healing. For over 25 years, she has had the privilege of studying with the best healers from all over the world, who have passed down ancient teachings on how to utilize energy technology. Heather is the author of *Crystal365*. In 2000, Heather co-founded Energy Muse with business partner Timmi. Timmi's background in sales and operations helps to make them a dynamic duo in this industry. Energy Muse is a conscious lifestyle brand, providing tools of empowerment, inspiration, and hope in the tangible form of jewelry and crystals. Together, Heather and Timmi are helping people reconnect with the energy of the Earth to align with their highest selves, realize their true calling, and tap into their own personal magnificence. You can visit them online at www.energymuse.com.

HAY HOUSE TITLES
OF RELATED INTEREST

YOU CAN HEAL YOUR LIFE,
the movie, starring Louise Hay & Friends
(available as a 1-DVD program, an expanded 2-DVD set,
and an online streaming video)
Learn more at www.hayhouse.com/louise-movie

THE SHIFT,
the movie, starring Dr. Wayne W. Dyer
(available as a 1-DVD program, an expanded 2-DVD set,
and an online streaming video)
Learn more at www.hayhouse.com/the-shift-movie

OWN YOUR GLOW:
A Soulful Guide to Luminous Living and Crowning the Queen Within,
by Latham Thomas

THE UNIVERSE HAS YOUR BACK:
Transform Fear to Faith,
by Gabrielle Bernstein

YOU HAVE 4 MINUTES TO CHANGE YOUR LIFE:
Simple 4-Minute Meditations for Inspiration,
Transformation, and True Bliss,
by Rebekah Borucki

---

*All of the above are available at your local bookstore,
or may be ordered by contacting Hay House
(see next page).*

We hope you enjoyed this Hay House book. If you'd like to receive our online catalog featuring additional information on Hay House books and products, or if you'd like to find out more about the Hay Foundation, please contact:

Hay House, Inc., P.O. Box 5100, Carlsbad, CA 92018-5100
(760) 431-7695 or (800) 654-5126
(760) 431-6948 (fax) or (800) 650-5115 (fax)
www.hayhouse.com® • www.hayfoundation.org

———

Published in Australia by: Hay House Australia Pty. Ltd.,
18/36 Ralph St., Alexandria NSW 2015
Phone: 612-9669-4299 • *Fax:* 612-9669-4144
www.hayhouse.com.au

Published in the United Kingdom by: Hay House UK, Ltd.,
The Sixth Floor, Watson House, 54 Baker Street, London W1U 7BU
Phone: +44 (0)20 3927 7290 • *Fax:* +44 (0)20 3927 7291
www.hayhouse.co.uk

Published in India by: Hay House Publishers India,
Muskaan Complex, Plot No. 3, B-2, Vasant Kunj, New Delhi 110 070
Phone: 91-11-4176-1620 • *Fax:* 91-11-4176-1630
www.hayhouse.co.in

———

Access New Knowledge.
Anytime. Anywhere.

Learn and evolve at your own pace
with the world's leading experts.

www.hayhouseU.com

Listen. Learn. Transform.

Listen to the audio version of this book for FREE!

Today, life is more hectic than ever—so you deserve on-demand and on-the-go solutions that inspire growth, center your mind, and support your well-being.

Introducing the *Hay House Unlimited Audio* mobile app. Now you can listen to this book (and countless others)—without having to restructure your day.

With your membership, you can:

- Enjoy over 30,000 hours of audio from your favorite authors.

- Explore audiobooks, meditations, Hay House Radio episodes, podcasts, and more.

- Listen anytime and anywhere with offline listening.

- Access exclusive audios you won't find anywhere else.

Try FREE for 7 days!